Impatiens

Impatiens

The Vibrant World of Busy Lizzies, Balsams, and Touch-me-nots

Raymond J. Morgan

Timber Press

Published in 2007 by
Timber Press, Inc.
The Haseltine Building
133 S.W. Second Avenue, Suite 450
Portland, Oregon 97204-3527, U.S.A.

www.timberpress.com

For contact information regarding editorial, marketing, sales, and
distribution in the United Kingdom, see www.timberpress.co.uk.

Designed by Christi Payne
Printed in China

Library of Congress Cataloging-in-Publication Data

Morgan, Raymond J.
    Impatiens : the vibrant world of Busy Lizzies, Balsams, and
Touch-me-nots / Raymond J. Morgan.
        p. cm.
    Includes bibliographical references and index.
    ISBN-13: 978-0-88192-852-5
  1. Impatiens. I. Title.
    QK495.B25M67 2007
    635.9'3379—dc22

2007019023

A catalog record for this book is also available from the British Library.

To my wife, Pamela, with my love

Contents

Foreword

I mpatiens, or balsams as they are popularly called today, have long fascinated me. When I was a botanist at the Royal Botanic Gardens Kew in the early 1970s, Professor Patrick Brenan, who was Keeper of the Herbarium, suggested that the genus *Impatiens*, particularly the African species, might make a suitable subject for my doctorate. He added that the last person to do any substantial work on them was the renowned Joseph Dalton Hooker, and that was in the latter part of the 19th century. My interest was fired, and I have been intrigued by them ever since.

In those days the only species commonly seen in cultivation was the East African *Impatiens walleriana* (or *I. sultanii*, as it was then called), while in gardens and the countryside the Himalayan balsam or policeman's helmet, *I. glandulifera*, had become a prodigious weed, albeit a very attractive one. I well remember being called in the late 1970s to see a consignment of balsams sent to Kew from New Guinea. The richness and size of the flowers and the shapes and colors of the leaves were remarkable, and it immediately struck me that here were plants of considerable horticultural value. In those days the New Guinea types were scarcely known, but how different is the situation today. For they, along with the African *I. walleriana*, are a multimillion-dollar business, with new forms and colors and a plethora of new cultivar and series names being produced each year by a number of seed houses.

Yet even today, of the thousand or so species known from the wild, very few are common in cultivation, although increasing numbers are finding their way into cultivation by one means or another. The great diversity of form and color found within the genus mark it out as one of huge potential both for the pot plant and container industry, while others will undoubtedly prove to be good hardy perennials for the garden. At the same time, the medicinal and other properties of these plants have scarcely begun to be explored.

It is, I suppose, the great diversity of flower shape that most intrigues me. Few genera exhibit such a variety of spur and petal shapes, whose patterns, ridges, and other features seem infinite. In this way impatiens rival some orchids in diversity and color, and like many orchids the evolution of the flower form is closely related to that of their pollinators.

Although there are various technical books and flora accounts of *Impatiens*, there is no general book for the gardener and plant-lover, so it is very pleasing to be able to write a foreword for Ray Morgan's book. I have known Ray for a number of years now and, although we have never actually met, we do speak regularly on the phone. Amateur horticulturists can sometimes prove a tiresome breed, but I soon realized that in Ray there was a person both passionate and dedicated to his subject and, in a relatively short time, he has amassed a large and impressive collection of balsams from around the world. In many ways, dedicated growers and collectors like Ray are the best people to establish such collections because they can specialize in a particular genus and, more importantly, devote plenty of time to their cultivation, something that few botanic gardens can afford to do because they are looking after huge collections of very diverse plants.

While the prospect of bringing a greater range of plants into cultivation is exciting, it must be emphasized that their status in the wild is of paramount importance. Plants cannot be brought into cultivation at any cost, particularly if it endangers their existence in the wild or breaks national or international laws. Impatiens, like many other plants, are under threat, particularly the many narrow-endemic species found in places like East Africa, Madagascar, India, and Sri Lanka. In a world increasingly under threat from development, these plants need to be admired and cherished. Ray Morgan's book will certainly help to raise awareness of, and appreciation for, these delightful and colorful plants.

Christopher Grey-Wilson

Christopher Grey-Wilson, Ph.D., is a botanist, horticulturist, and author who is currently the editor of *The Alpine Garden Society*.

Preface

I t is no exaggeration to say that impatiens are the first choice for summer planting everywhere. The very mention of impatiens to most gardeners brings to mind patio pots and window boxes filled with color. Parks and city centers all over the world are aflame with their flowers throughout the summer months.

Until relatively recently impatiens were grown primarily as greenhouse pot plants. Since the early 1980s, however, their popularity has rocketed to a point where they now top the list of best-selling plants at garden centers. With the rise in interest of patio gardening, impatiens are now regarded as indispensable for use in all forms of containers and hanging baskets. Although the individual flowers may not last very long, the plants more than make up for this by their prolific flowering capacity.

The common name "busy Lizzie" is usually associated with just one species, *Impatiens walleriana*, a plant that has been extensively hybridized and refined into the multitude of colors we have today, so much so that *I. walleriana* is now cultivated throughout the gardening world. To these the New Guinea hybrids have been added, with their even more flamboyant flowers, some over 7 cm across, often with the addition of variegated leaf coloration. Virtually unknown before 1970, the New Guinea hybrids (crosses with *I. hawkeri*) also have secured their place on the sales benches of garden centers. Finally, there is *I. balsamina*, a plant that has been cultivated for centuries and was once a cottage-garden favorite, but sadly in recent times has been a little overlooked.

Impatiens walleriana, the New Guinea hybrids (*I. hawkeri* group), *I. balsamina*, and *I. glandulifera* are the only impatiens to have been cultivated to any great extent, but there are hundreds more *Impatiens* species growing in the wild and relatively unknown to horticulture. In this book I describe *Impatiens* species from across Africa and Asia, as well as the islands off the shores of these continents. Some of these plants would make great additions to the gardens of the future. Many nurseries are already offering some of them, and more are being added to their catalogues all the time. If you are among those adventurous gardeners looking to try something different, impatiens have much to offer. They are easy to cultivate, grow in a wide range of soils, adapt to shade or full sun, and provide a profusion of flowers throughout the summer months. I am confident that you will find them most rewarding.

Acknowledgments

My grateful thanks to the following people for contributing so much help and encouragement, as well as photographs: Derick Pitman, Dr. Eberhard Fischer, Dr. Yong-Ming Yuan, Chuyos Punpreuk, Dr. Tarrun Chaabra, Michael Ferrero, Dr. Brian Corr (Ball Horticultural), Birgit Hofmann (Fischers), and Silvia Hofmann (Innova Plant).

Introduction

The genus *Impatiens* belongs to the family Balsaminaceae in the order Geraniales, which also includes the genera *Geranium, Pelargonium, Oxalis,* and *Tropaeolum*. Current estimates put the number of *Impatiens* species at more than 1000, which makes it surprising that so few have found their way into cultivation. Apart from *I. walleriana, I. hawkeri* (that is, the New Guinea hybrids), *I. glandulifera,* and *I. balsamina,* very few other species are being grown, except within the confines of botanical gardens. The situation is changing, however, as today's gardener is constantly searching for new and unusual plants to grow.

The genus *Impatiens* is so named because of the explosive nature of the seed capsule. When ripe, the capsule ejects its seed with great force at the slightest touch, suggesting its impatience to restart growth. This phenomenon is caused by the contraction of elastic valves of the capsule. It is a feature of every species in the genus and a reason why many have acquired the name "touch-me-not."

Impatiens balsamina

Carl Linnaeus described seven *Impatiens* species in his *Species Plantarum* (1753), including *Impatiens balsamina,* from which the family Balsaminaceae takes its name. This species has been in cultivation for centuries and can be found growing in many parts of Asia. Apart from its floral attributes, *I.*

balsamina has been used medicinally for centuries. Its soothing properties have been used to treat a variety of ailments, in much the same way as the ancients did with balms or balsams, thus explaining the origin of the epithet *balsamina* and the common name "balsam."

Nearly all impatiens are endemic to tropical, subtropical, and temperate parts of Africa, Madagascar, and Asia, particularly in India, China, and Southeast Asia, with a few species in Europe and North America. Most *Impatiens* species, however, are generally restricted in their geographic distribution. For instance, few Himalayan species are found in both the eastern and western parts of the range, and apart from *Impatiens balsamina*, there are no other Himalayan species to be found in southern India. No African species occur naturally anywhere in Asia and vice versa.

Although most impatiens come from the warmer regions of the world, nearly all are found at elevations between 1000 and 3000 m, where the cooler temperatures are more favorable for their growth. The genus is composed of annuals and perennials, but there are no known biennial species. Most of the African species are perennial, as are many of the southern Indian and virtually all the East Indies species. Throughout a good deal of the temperate regions, including the Himalayas, northern India, and Nepal, there is a predominance of annual species, although there is still a sizable portion of perennials, mainly in the more easterly parts of the Himalayas and China.

With few exceptions, impatiens prefer a damp, shady environment near rivers or streams and among mosses and ferns. A few species grow epiphytically on the branches of trees, taking sustenance from accumulated leaf litter and forest debris. Some impatiens find a home in the cracks and crevices of rocks, in little pockets of humus, or in river- or streambanks, sometimes even growing in the streams during periods of high rainfall.

Impatiens species show a wide diversity of sizes, shapes, flower colors, and habit of growth, ranging from ground hugging, trailing plants to tall, erect herbs that can grow to 3 m high. Some impatiens are shrublike, some are semi-aquatic, and there are epiphytes, lithophytes, and even a few species that are described as caudiform succulents. There is a great deal of variation within each species as well, but remarkably little natural hybridization between them.

A good deal of interest was shown in *Impatiens* in the early part of the 19th century, as new species were continually being discovered. Botanists such as Robert Wight, Richard Henry Beddome, Michael Pakenham Edgeworth, and Nathaniel Wallich made plant-hunting expeditions to many parts of the world, discovering hundreds of new plants, including many *Impatiens* species. In 1896 George Bentham and Joseph Dalton Hooker produced *Genera Plantarum*, a work classifying and describing botanically all the known plants at that time. Their classifications soon became known as the Bentham and Hooker system.

Sir Joseph Dalton Hooker (1817–1911) was the son of William Jackson Hooker, the first director of the Royal Botanic Gardens at Kew. Joseph succeeded his father as the garden's director in 1865, and he remained in the position until 1885. J. D. Hooker made many botanical expeditions to various parts of the world. In 1848 he led one to the central and eastern Himalayas, at that time unmapped and untraveled by Europeans. During the expedition, Hooker collected great numbers of plants, including *Rhododendron* and *Impatiens* species, and produced the first accurate map of the region. Together with Charles Henry Thompson, Hooker made the initial survey of the genus *Impatiens* in 1859. In the *Flora of British India* (1874–1875), Hooker classified and described 120 Indian species. During the last decade of his life, he spent a great deal of his time updating his previous work, and in 1904–1906 Hooker published "An Epitome of British Indian Species of Impatiens," in which he added many more new species.

Sir Joseph Dalton Hooker
Reproduced with the kind permission of the Director of the Board of Trustees, Royal Botanic Gardens, Kew

After Hooker's work, no great strides were made, except by regional studies, until Christopher Grey-Wilson's *Impatiens of Africa* was published in 1980. This work classifies and describes all the known African species in great detail and has become the definitive work on the subject.

Impatiens walleriana, the species commonly known as "busy Lizzie," comes to us from Africa. It was introduced into cultivation in 1896 from the island of Zanzibar, under the name *I. sultanii*, in honor of the sultan of that island, who had been instrumental in eradicating the slavery trade from this part of eastern Africa. The plant also grows in Kenya, Mozambique, and Malawi and has been known variously as *I. holstii*, *I. hopsii*, and *I. walleriana*. Grey-Wilson grouped them all under the single name of *I. walleriana*, however, due to the fact that that this plant had been described by Hooker in a collection made in 1868.

Impatiens walleriana is a perennial species but is often grown as an annual. It flowers abundantly from May until the first frosts. Under glass and with a little heat, it can be continuously flowering, and under favorable light conditions this species will make a fine flowering houseplant. In the garden or patio *I. walleriana* is increasingly being used as a container, window box, and hanging basket subject. The color range is bewildering, in shades of red, pink, orange, salmon, lilac, mauve, and white, with starburst, picotee-edged, and mosaic patterning. Add to this the double and semi-double varieties, and it is easy to see how *I. walleriana* has become arguably the world's most popular flowering plant. The choice has been increased by the introduction of variegated single and double forms, with white- or cream-splashed green leaves, which seem to make the flowers stand out even more. Recent novelties such as the Firefly and Mini Hawaiian series have been appearing, so there is something here to please everyone.

Vying for first place among impatiens are the New Guinea hybrids developed by crossing different varieties of *Impatiens hawkeri*, which has resulted in more spectacular and colorful flowers, as well as leaf coloration. *Impatiens hawkeri* is native to New Guinea and the surrounding islands, where it has been grown for generations by the Papuans. They collect and trade the plants, actively selecting the showier varieties and planting them in and around their villages for decorative effect. Although *I. hawkeri* has been in general culture since 1886, it was not until 1970 that the species was crossed with other varieties from the region to produce these wonderful hybrids, with the pioneering work carried out mainly in the United States. By using other species from Sulawesi (formerly Celebes) and Java, crosses have been made to create hundreds of new hybrids, with huge flowers up to 7 cm across and in a wider color range (see chapter 4).

Impatiens hawkeri has a different growth habit than that of *I. walleriana*, being rather more upright in stature and growing into a much larger plant, up to 1 m tall. Its leaves are arranged in distinct whorls, often with attractive coloration. This plant has been known under such names as *I. herzogii*, *I. mooreana*, and *I. schlecteri*. Although all these names are synonyms of *I. hawkeri*, they are best looked upon as varieties. *Impatiens herzogii* is a glabrous plant with vermilion flowers; *I. mooreana* has green leaves and pink flowers; *I. schlecteri* has dark bronze, narrow or lanceolate leaves and red flowers; and *I. hawkeri* has broad green leaves and magenta flowers. They can be grown from seed, but the best plants are propagated from cuttings. Apart from a few annual species such as *I. balsamina*, *I. walleriana* and the New Guinea hybrids are the only impatiens grown to any extent.

With one or two exceptions, *Impatiens* are plants of the Old World, and no species have been found in South America, Australia, or New Zealand. North America has two indigenous species, *I. capensis* and *I. pallida*, while Britain has only one, *I. noli-tangere*, which can be found growing in the north of Eng-

Impatiens capensis

Impatiens pallida

Impatiens glandulifera

land, Norfolk, and north Wales. *Impatiens noli-tangere* was first discovered by George Bowles in 1632 and was mentioned in *Gerard's Herbal* (1634) as growing in Shropshire, near the Welsh border, where it can still be found today. It was one of the original balsam species described by Linnaeus, and its name literally means "do not touch." This species is a pretty, yellow-flowered plant with glaucous leaves, growing to about 1 m high. The plant prefers a damp shady habitat and grows near rivers or streams. Although still a rather rare plant in Britain, *I. noli-tangere* can be found growing across Europe, into Asia, and to the Far East.

Several Himalayan species have become naturalized over parts of the United States and Europe, including *Impatiens parviflora*, *I. balfourii*, and *I. glandulifera*. First introduced to Europe from Nepal in 1838, *I. glandulifera* quickly became a garden favorite. In fact, J. D. Hooker was known to have grown it in his own garden. It was not long before *I. glandulifera* acquired its more common names of "Himalayan balsam" or "policeman's helmet" because of the flower's resemblance to this particular headwear. The species' energetic method of seed dispersal, however, soon led it to escape from the confinement of the garden and out into the surrounding land. It gradually colonized many parts of the English countryside, eventually spreading to parts of Europe. The same occurred in North America. It has now become one of Britain's best-loved wildflowers, yet one of the most troublesome; once established, *I. glandulifera* can take over large areas of damp land near rivers and can be difficult to control. In Nepal *I. glandulifera* seeds are often harvested as a food source. The seeds are pressed, and the extracted oil is used for cooking. The seeds are said to be nutritious and have a pleasant nutty taste.

Impatiens glandulifera is a plant of tremendous vigor that self-seeds prolifically, traits that lead it to be very invasive. It can grow to well over 2 m high and produces flowers in all shades of pink and purple. Its close relative, the pure white-flowered *I. candida*, makes a fine garden plant, just right for a place in back of the border. Although just as invasive, this variety is well worth growing and is easy enough to keep under control.

The two North American species, *I. capensis* and *I. pallida*, are perhaps better known under their common names of "jewelweed," "spotted touch-me-not," and "pale touch-me-not." The name "jewelweed" derives from the fact that the leaves repel moisture; raindrops or heavy dew settling on them form perfectly round droplets, which glisten like polished gemstones. *Impatiens capensis* has become naturalized in many locations across North America, chiefly in the more eastern United States and north into Canada, whereas *I. pallida* has a more regional distribution. These species can be found growing in many habitats from damp, marshy ground to the edges of shady woodland. Apart from the flowers, both plants look alike, growing to about 1 m in height, with rather glaucous foliage. *Impatiens capensis* has orange flowers heavily spotted with red, although it can sometimes be found in an unspotted, yellow form and occasionally with creamy white flowers. *Impatiens pallida* has pale lemon yellow, unspotted flowers.

The garden balsam, *Impatiens balsamina*, was the first *Impatiens* species to be cultivated, and records show that it has been grown for many centuries. It grows to 1 m in height and carries its large flowers close to the stem. *Impatiens balsamina* has been hybridized extensively and can be found in a wide range of colors, including all shades of pink, red, mauve, lilac, and white. Both single and double camellia-flowered forms, as well as dwarf varieties, are also available. *Impatiens balsamina* originated in India, but has become very widespread and is now found in most Asian countries. The seed of *I. balsamina* has a fairly long viability, which may account for its widespread distribution.

Several *Impatiens* species are believed to have medicinal properties. For instance, *I. balsamina* has been used for centuries in herbal remedies, mainly in China, for alleviating such diverse conditions as sickness caused from eating poisonous fish to the treatment of snakebites. The lower part of the stem, when pounded into a juice and added to rice liquor, is supposed to help reduce swelling and bruising of the skin. The dried stem is often ground into a paste and made into an ointment that relieves pain. The flowers are also crushed and made into a paste that is mucilaginous and cooling and can be used to treat lumbago and neuralgia. In Vietnam, a concoction of *I. balsamina* is used for washing hair and is supposed to promote its growth. In the Philippines, the leaves of other species are used as a poultice for healing wounds. In the United States, both *I. capensis* and *I. pallida* leaves are used to alleviate the painful symptoms of poison ivy. Alcoholic extracts of the flowers are supposed to possess a marked antibiotic activity against certain pathogenic fungi and bacteria. Medical research into the properties of other *Impatiens* species may yet prove to be fruitful.

Morphology of Impatiens

Impatiens are primarily plants of montane regions, usually found growing at elevations in excess of 1000 m, in damp, shady woodland habitats. Most impatiens do not do well at temperatures above 25°C (77°F). These mountainous habitats have led to many species becoming isolated due to the effects of landslides, erosion, and other topographical changes. Such isolation has been one of the major contributing factors in the evolution of so many different species in the genus. In addition, habitats at lower elevations, with their much warmer climatic conditions, form an effective barrier against the plants becoming more widely distributed. These barriers are the prime reason why so many of *Impatiens* species are endemic to a single location.

There is enormous variation in plant characteristics within the genera. The plants range in height from no more than 8–10 cm to the giant Himalayan *Impatiens glandulifera* at up to 3 m high. Most are of a somewhat succulent nature, although a few shrubby and subshrubby species exist. They can be upright, single-stemmed plants or greatly branched, trailing plants, often rooting where they touch the ground, forming rhizomatous mats above or below the soil level. In general, impatiens are moisture-loving plants, nearly always found growing near rivers and streams or otherwise boggy ground. They are intolerant of dry conditions and readily discard older, yellowing leaves to lessen the rate of transpiration. This partial defoliation occurs in a great many species. Some can become almost leafless, but for a few straggling leaves at the top of the plant, leaving their stems bare except for the scars of the fallen leaves.

Some *Impatiens* species have a tuberous rootstock, like that of dahlias. These are mostly deciduous, as in the African *I. tinctoria* and *I. flanaganae*, which lose their leaves in the long dry season. Others such as the Indian *I. acaulis* and *I. scapiflora* grow from little corms, much like cyclamen. The stemless, radical leaves and scaped flowers arise from underground, forming loose rosettes. These also die back at the onset of winter and re-emerge in late spring, after the rains, to start a new growth cycle.

Apart from this last group, the leaves of impatiens are presented around the stem in three distinct arrangements. Most conform to an alternate or spiral system, having a single leaf at each node. Others have opposing pairs of leaves at each node. Finally, some have leaves arranged in whorls or verticils of three to eight leaves displayed around a single node. Some species, however, exhibit two or even all three forms, starting life with an opposite arrangement and progressing to a spiral or to a whorled formation as the plant matures. The leaves themselves also display great variation in form and size and can have surfaces that range from shiny to completely tomentose. The one thing all have in common is that the leaf margins (edges) have some sort of crenulations or serrations, which range from quite pronounced to a bit obscure.

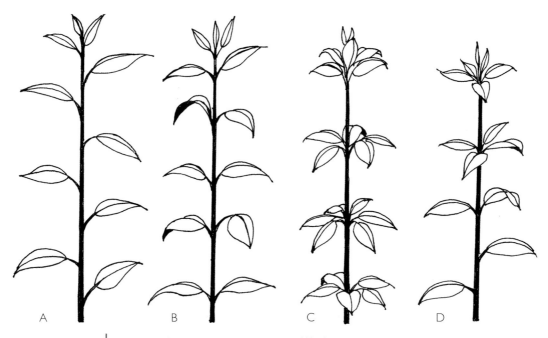

Fig. 1. Leaf arrangements in *Impatiens*: (A) alternate, (B) opposite, (C) verticillate, (D) a combination

In common with many other genera, *Impatiens* species often display stipular glands (extrafloral nectaries), usually positioned on or near the stem, at the base of the leaf, or at the junction of the petiole and the stem. Although quite small, they secrete tiny amounts of sweet, sticky nectar. These extrafloral nectaries project from the nodes in a variety of shapes and sizes. In some species, they can be found on the basal edges of the leaves or on the petiole itself. The function of the extrafloral nectaries is not clearly understood, as their presence seems to be detrimental to the plants reproductive mechanism by offering an alternative source of nectar for pollinating insects. Ants seem to find the nectar irresistible, however, suggesting a possible symbiotic relationship, with the ants distracting other potentially more troublesome insects.

The flowers of impatiens are so diverse that they rival the orchid family for variety, with their colors spanning the whole of the spectrum, perhaps more so than any other genus. The flowers fall mainly into two groups, one presenting a rather open faced, flat shape, typical of *Impatiens walleriana*, and the other being more cupped and elongated, typical of the "policeman's

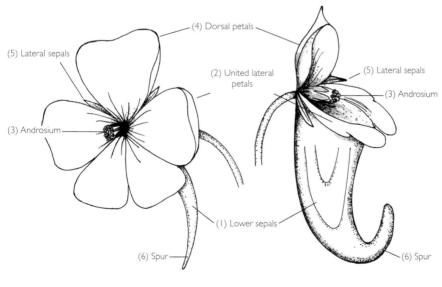

Flat open faced flower   Pouched flower

Fig. 2. Typical flower structures of *Impatiens*: (1) lower sepal, (2) united lateral petals, (3) androecium, (4) dorsal petal, (5) lateral sepals, (6) spur

helmet." The flat flowers usually face upward and are endowed with long, thin spurs that contain the nectar. Butterflies and moths are the only pollinators with a proboscis long enough to reach the nectary at the base of the spur. In contrast, the pouched flowers are held vertically and are nearly always pollinated by bees and wasps. These flowers are more complex, with the lateral petals usually extending outward to form a lip, providing a platform on which a bee can alight to gain easier access into the flower.

Broadly speaking, the flower consists of five sepals and five petals, but in the vast majority of *Impatiens* species the sepals are reduced to just three. The two lateral sepals are positioned one on either side of the flower and are usually small. In most cases the extra pair will be missing or greatly reduced in size. The remaining sepal is positioned at the bottom of the flower; it is always much larger than the others and modified into a horn or pouch-shaped structure. This sepal can be long and filiform, ending in a spur that contains the nectar, or inflated into a large pouch, with the spur constricted at the end into a narrow incurving appendage, this being one of the major identifying characteristics. The dorsal (standard or flag) petal is positioned at the top, with a pair of lateral petals at either side. These lateral petals show enormous variation in their shape, but they are always united to some degree at the base and are often referred to as the wings. In addition, some species have a dorsal auricle, an appendage on the inside edge of the lowermost lateral petal, which takes various forms. The purpose of the dorsal auricle is not clearly understood, but again it is thought to be involved in pollination.

The flowers of all *Impatiens* species are zygomorphic (that is, bilaterally symmetrical), meaning they have only one plane of symmetry by which they can be divided into two equal halves. (In the case of nonzygomorphic flowers, such as dahlias, chrysanthemums, and marigolds, a cut across the center in any direction would show complete symmetry.) *Impatiens* flowers are also resupinate; that is, they are twisted through 180° at the pedicel, so that in reality they are viewed upside down. Resupination also occurs in many orchid species, the effect being to place the spur at the base of the flower, allowing easier access for the pollinating insect to the nectar contained within.

The flowers have five anthers and stamens, which are closely grouped and fused together to form the androecium, arranged around a five-celled stigma that protrudes downward. The back of the pollinating insect brushes against it, dislodging some of the pollen, or if the stigma underneath is ripe, the insect may dislodge the androecium as a complete unit to expose the stigma beneath, allowing pollination by some other insect to take place.

All *Impatiens* species are bisexual. The flowers have a male stage in which the anthers are displayed, usually for only a short time (from a few days to perhaps only a few hours); they then lose the anther covering, exposing the female stigma. Some species, however, are able to self-fertilize. Many high-elevation annuals have this ability, possibly brought about by the scarcity of pollinating insects. Self-fertilization is achieved by the ripening stigma ejecting the combined anther-stamen unit, which often does not break away cleanly, allowing some of the pollen to fall onto the stigma and thereby effecting pollination.

Some species have evolved a quite different approach to self-pollination. For instance, the North American *Impatiens capensis* produces two very different types of buds: a normal one that opens to offer itself to pollinating insects and another bud that only produces embryonic flowers with tiny amounts of pollen and no nectar. This second bud progresses directly from bud to seed capsule, without ever displaying a flower, a process known as cleistogamy. The resultant capsule only produces a small amount of seed, but enough to ensure continuity of the species. The *I. capensis* plant uses up a good deal of energy in producing pollen in the normal flowers. Therefore, by producing cleistogamous buds a stunted plant does not need to expend so much energy in order to reproduce. Cleistogamy also occurs in a few Madagascan *Impatiens* species and in many other genera as well. Only annual species are known to produce cleistogamous buds. This alternative reproductive process is more evident when growth conditions are not optimum. For instance, normal growth sometimes becomes stunted during dry periods, so the plant produces many more of the cleistogamous buds to assure continuity. On occasion, these buds are produced before the normal flowering time, sometimes prior to a long dry season that may be likely to kill off the plants before they can produce the normal, chasmogamous flowers.

The inflorescence of *Impatiens* shows a good deal of diversity, ranging from single flowers or pairs to large racemes or umbels of many dozen blooms. An axillary inflorescence is comprised of a pedicel rising from the junction between the leaf petiole and the stem, whereas in a terminal inflorescence the pedicel is produced at the top of the stem. The pedicel can then split into a number of flower stalks (peduncles), at the base of which are tiny modified leaves or bracts of various shapes and sizes. In some species, such as *I. balsamina*, the flowers are borne with no pedicel and are said to be epedunculate. At the other extreme, the inflorescence of *I. radiata* has sprays of dozens of flowers.

Variation of seed capsules: (upper left) linear capsule of *Impatiens namchabarwensis*, (upper right) spindle-shaped capsule of *I. auricoma*, (lower left) club-shaped capsule of *I. glandulifera*, and (lower right) linear capsule of *I. scabrida*.

The seed capsules fall mainly into two groups: fusiform and linear. The fusiform capsule is short, spindle-shaped, and pointed at either end and becomes turgid at the center with age. The fusiform seed capsule is typified by *Impatiens walleriana*, as well as almost all the African species and most of the tropical ones. Those with linear capsules are mainly species of the temperate regions, such as *I. scabrida* and *I. balfourii*. Seed capsules may also be clavate (club-shaped), as in *I. glandulifera*, or even hooked or beak-shaped, as in *I. maculata* and *I. viscida*. In all *Impatiens* species, however, the common factor is that they eject their seeds explosively, sometimes for many meters in all directions.

The method of dehiscence (seed dispersal) is different in the two major types of seed capsules. In the short fusiform capsule, five elastic longitudinal sections encase the seed, which are distributed along its length. Dehiscence is carried out in two distinct motions. When ripe, the capsule becomes turgid in the middle and great tension is built up within. One of the sections splits open at the center, then rips equally toward each end. The dehisced seeds are then thrown out at great speed as the remaining sections collapse, rapidly rolling in on each other toward the center. In the linear capsule, the bottom portion is composed of five elastic sections but usually no seed, whereas the top portion has seed but no elasticity. The linear capsule splits from the bottom up, with the sections simultaneously rolling up toward the apex so rapidly that the membranous portion at the top is torn to pieces, ejecting the seed in all directions in one complete motion.

2

Taxonomy and Hybridization

Since Carl Linnaeus described seven *Impatiens* species in his *Species Plantarum* in 1753, more than 1000 species have been described by taxonomists. During their numerous expeditions throughout Africa, Asia, and the islands of the Indian Ocean, plant hunters have also discovered a few naturally occurring hybrids.

Impatiens Taxonomy

The discovery of a completely new species is covered by the International Code of Botanical Nomenclature, which has laid down specific rules concerning new taxa. First, a new species has to be described in Latin and published in a reputable book or botanical journal. A type specimen has to be obtained, dry pressed, and placed in the care of a recognized herbarium, with extra notes on the type locality, and, if possible, pollinators along with illustrations, preferably in color.

In the case of most genera, this system works quite well. Unfortunately, the succulent nature of most impatiens means that they do not make ideal herbarium specimens, making comparative identification quite difficult. Most of the plants are soft, with high moisture content, particularly the flowers. When dried and pressed, they become membranous and rather brittle. Therefore, some *Impatiens* herbarium specimens are found to be incomplete and lacking in important diagnostic components.

Herbarium specimen

In the 19th century, numerous *Impatiens* species were collected and described, and many of these were thought to be completely new discoveries. With the difficulty in comparing the specimens, some species have been described more than once, and on the odd occasion, two completely different species have been described and given the same name, confounding the issue even more. In fact, J. D. Hooker stated, "In no genus of flowering plants known to me, is the difficulty of analyzing herbarium specimens so great." As a consequence, some *Impatiens* species have been known by various names. In these cases, the first described takes precedence over the rest, with its other names becoming synonyms.

For instance, for a great many years the busy Lizzie was known to gardeners by various names, including *Impatiens walleriana*, *I. sultanii*, and *I. holstii*. The name *I. walleriana* was given in honor of Horace Waller, the botanist who first collected the plant while accompanying Dr. David Livingstone on his first expedition to eastern Africa. The specimen was subsequently described by J. D. Hooker in 1868 in Daniel Oliver's *Flora of Tropical Africa*. *Impatiens sultanii*, the variant from eastern Africa, was discovered by the naturalist Sir John Kirk in Zanzibar. *Impatiens sultanii* was also described by J. D. Hooker in 1882 in the *Curtis Botanical Magazine*. (The name is still used today by some seed merchants.) In 1895 the variant *I. holstii*, a very floriferous form with bright red flowers, was discovered in the Usambra and Kilimanjari Mountains. This variant was described by Heinrich Gustav Adolf Engler in 1921 in *Planzenwelt Afrikas*. All of these variants, however, have now been subsumed into the species *I. walleriana*.

As an aid to the classification of species, we owe botanical artists a great deal. The illustrations that have appeared in botanical books and journals over the years make identification clearer than any written description. Some of these illustrations are works of art in their own right, and the work of artists such as Walter Hood Fitch and Matilda Smith during the late 19th century was quite superb. Much of

A 19th-century drawing by Walter Wood Fitch of *Impatiens repens*, a trailing species from Sri Lanka

An undescribed *Impatiens* from the Himalayan region of China

their work, including some illustrations of *Impatiens* species, was published in periodicals such as the *Curtis Botanical Magazine* and the *Kew Magazine*. Many of the great names in botany were also gifted illustrators. The botanist Robert Wight beautifully illustrated many Indian *Impatiens* species, as far back as 1820. In their time, W. J. Hooker and J. D. Hooker were excellent botanical artists, and the contemporary botanist Christopher Grey-Wilson has illustrated most of the African *Impatiens* species, as well as many from other parts of the world.

With a genus of more than a 1000 species, identification clearly becomes a great problem. Many attempts have been made at grouping the individual species according to specific characteristics, such as leaf arrangement, flower shape and color, or seed capsule. Classification remains difficult, however, because *Impatiens* is a large and diverse genus, with many species showing a good deal of variation. Because the genus has a widespread distribution, *Impatiens* is primarily classified by region, for instance, the African, Indian, and Himalayan species. They are then reduced by a system of grouping or keying, usually based on vegetative characteristics. Within each region, this key system works quite well, but it becomes unwieldy as a universal system.

In addition, several taxonomists have developed their own individual keys for the various regions, based on different criteria.

One important characteristic of all *Impatiens* is the seed capsule. Most of the African and Southeast Asian species, almost all of which are perennial, bear a fusiform seed capsule. Those with a linear capsule are mostly species found in the more temperate regions, including the Himalayas, China, and northern India, with a few from Europe and North America. Variations of the linear capsule include clavate and beaked seed capsules. One species that stands out from nearly all others is *I. balsamina*, in having a large, spindle-shaped, tomentose (hairy) capsule. Although this was the first species to have been described, it stands alone in having a tomentose seed capsule.

When dealing with *Impatiens*, most present-day taxonomists follow Grey-Wilson's classification used in his work on African species. Much of the recent taxonomic work has been carried out by the Japanese botanists Shinobu Akiyama, Hideaki Ohba, and Michio Wakabayashi, working in the main from universities in Kyoto and Tokyo. Their work has been centered around the Himalayan species, clarifying some of the classification that has always

An unidentified *Impatiens* from northern India

been a little obscure. In addition, Hiroshi Hara and Tatemi Shimitzu have concentrated mainly on the species growing in the Himalayas and Thailand, respectively. Chinese ecologists have increasingly been focusing on conservation. Botanists such as S. H. Huang and Y. L. Chan have been prominent in this field, and they have discovered and described dozens of new *Impatiens* species from Yunnan and Sichuan Provinces. In Africa and Madagascar, botanists such as Eberhard Fischer have been in the forefront of discovering new species and have recently described a great many new ones.

Indian botanists also have become increasingly aware of their indigenous species and have been initiating plant protection schemes. Much of their work has involved collecting endangered species and relocating them to more protected areas. During this process, previously undescribed impatiens are sometimes found. Because India can boast more than 200 *Impatiens* species, identification is very important and classification needs to be precise. Currently there is a good deal of this work being carried out in southwestern India. The Flora of India Botanical Survey is in the process of classifying all Indian flora, with botanists establishing a census of *Impatiens* species. Some recent finds have included species last recorded as far back as 1930. Unfortunately, other Indian species appear to have gone extinct due to the loss of habitat to the needs of agriculture and forestry development.

Impatiens Hybrids in the Wild

Considering the very wide diversity within the genus *Impatiens*, it seems surprising to find that there are so few naturally occurring hybrids. There are a few notable exceptions, however. When the species grow in close proximity, *I. kilimanjari* has been known to hybridize with *I. pseudoviola*, sometimes forming quite large hybrid colonies. Similarly *I. gomphophylla* has crossed with *I. austrotanzanica*, forming a range of hybrids with different flower colors, as well as with *I. polyantha*. The western Himalayan *I. balfourii*, which also grows abundantly in Pakistan, has been shown to hybridize with *I. pseudobicolor*, from the same region, forming large hybrid colonies in the wild.

Hybrid plants resulting from the cross *I. walleriana* × *I. usambarensis* are found growing in northern Tanzania. *Impatiens usambarensis* is endemic to this area, whereas *I. walleriana* was introduced there over the years by gardeners, who transplanted it from other locations in the country. Because these two species have similar pollinators, it was just a matter of time before the cross occurred.

There are several reasons for this scarcity of natural hybrids. First, *Impatiens* species generally tend to be endemic to a particular location, so that geographic barriers prevent hybridization between species. In addition, individual species usually have specialist pollinators, so that pollen is not exchanged between the flowers of different species. Many species are pollinated by bees, others by butterflies and moths, and some are even pollinated by small birds. In Africa, tiny sunbirds are attracted to the red flowers of some species. Colonies of different species growing close enough to one another for potential hybridization to occur may have quite different natural pollinators, likely due to differences in flower shape or color. Under cultivated conditions, some crosses can be accomplished through hand-pollination. The main reason for the scarcity of natural hybrids, however, is that of genetic incompatibility due to the numerous mutations that have arisen in each species over the course of their evolution.

*Impatiens
pseudoviola* ×
I. kilimanjari hybrid

*Impatiens
pseudoviola
× I. kilimanjari
hybrid 2*

*Impatiens
pseudoviola
× I. kilimanjari
hybrid 3*

3

Impatiens Breeding Programs

fter the introduction of impatiens to Western horticulture in the late 19th century, the species were grown almost exclusively as greenhouse pot plants. Because impatiens flower prolifically, are some of the easiest plants to grow, and perform well in a variety of conditions from full sun to deep shade, they have now become one of our top bedding plants and are used extensively in gardens and parks throughout the world to create displays of nonstop color. Breeders have worked to increase the size and color range of the flowers and have produced cultivars with variegated foliage and trailing habits.

In recent years the growth of the horticultural trade worldwide has been nothing less than phenomenal, generating many millions of dollars annually. The main focus has been on the sale of spring annual bedding and patio plants. A huge portion of this business is attributable to the sale of impatiens in the form of *Impatiens walleriana* and the New Guinea hybrids, sold as both potted plants and plugs or tray-grown plants. To keep this momentum going, the breeding of new and interesting additions is essential. This fact has got the interest of most of the larger plant producers, and consequently they are working hard to satisfy this need.

In the wild, the African species *Impatiens walleriana* shows a very wide range of variation of form and color, and plant breeders have capitalized on this natural variation to bring us the wonderful range of plants that are on offer today. More than any other, this species has held the attention of the horticultural world for many years, and a great deal of work has been carried out in refining it into the position it now holds as the most widely sold bedding plant. The New Guinea species have been cross-bred into hundreds of colorful hybrids. Work on other species has also shown promising results.

Impatiens 'African Orchid'

Hand-pollinated crosses between the African *I. kilimanjari* and *I. pseudoviola* have produced some remarkably colorful hybrids. Crosses between the Madagascan species *I. auricoma* and *I. tuberosa* yielded *Impatiens* 'African Orchid'. The flowers have the same shape as those of *I. auricoma* but come in a wide range of pastel colors and many bicolors. These hybrids are easy to cultivate and can be grown from seed; the best selections can be kept for growing on by propagating from cuttings.

Many other interspecific crosses also have been made, although in most cases the resultant hybrids showed little improvement over the parents and were often found to be sterile. In 1970 Dr. Toru Arisumi of the U.S. Department of Agriculture carried out a great deal of work on interspecific breeding with *Impatiens* species that were generally considered to be incompatible. His method involved the use of bridge hybrids, which he obtained by hand-pollinating a variety of different species. Only a few of the crosses were successful, but he managed to grow these few to the flowering stage. Most were sterile, however, meaning that the problem of sterility had to be overcome to make further crosses. Arisumi achieved this by the use of the alkaloid colchicine, which inhibits mitosis and doubles the chromosome count. Tiny amounts of colchicine were introduced to the growing tips of the hybrids,

Impatiens 'Tangerine' (Seashell series)

which increased the chance of fertile crosses due to the greater amount of genetic material allowing for a match. By using the pollen from these intermediary, now fertile hybrids, Arisumi was eventually able to make successful crosses with different species. Another problem was that many of these interspecific hybrids produced seed capsules that were prone to abort before reaching maturity. Arisumi devised a procedure known as embryo rescue, in which he was able to remove the immature seed to grow in an agar gel solution in the laboratory. This process of growing whole plants from a few immature cells, called micropropagation, led to new hybrids such as the Seashell series.

Impatiens auricoma is one of the parents of the Seashell series, which have completely new flower colors including yellow, apricot, tangerine, and papaya, an orange-red. All have the same habit as *I. walleriana*, the other parent, but the flowers are slightly cup-shaped. In rainy regions, the colors of the Seashell series do not seem to hold very well, and often they appear washed out. When grown in the greenhouse, however, they hold their colors much better.

Using micropropagation techniques, Ball Horticultural introduced an improvement on these *Impatiens auricoma* × *I. walleriana* hybrids. Cultivars within the Fusion series hold their flower colors better than the Seashell

Impatiens 'Radiance' (Fusion series)
Ball Horticultural

Impatiens 'Heat' (Fusion series)
Ball Horticultural

Impatiens 'Sunset' (Fusion series)
Ball Horticultural

Impatiens 'Glow' (Fusion series)
Ball Horticultural

Impatiens 'Glow' (Fusion series)
Ball Horticultural

hybrids. The Fusion series includes the peach-colored 'Radiance', the orange-red 'Heat', the yellow-flowered 'Glow', the pinkish red 'Infrared', and the apricot-colored 'Sunset'. The flowers are a little more open faced than the Seashell series and are more like the normal *I. walleriana*.

In recent years, plant laboratories around the world have been using micropropagation to create new and exciting hybrids. For instance, the German

Impatiens 'Bufly Saley' (Butterfly series)
Vernons

firm of Fischers developed the Butterfly series of hybrids by making crosses between *Impatiens pseudoviola* and *I. walleriana*. The flowers are a little smaller than those of *I. walleriana*, but they are produced in an abundance. The plants have a trailing habit, making them ideal for large planters and hanging baskets.

Crosses between the Sri Lankan species *Impatiens repens* and *I. walleriana* have so far been a little disappointing, due to the fact that the gene controlling the yellow flower color in *I. repens* is recessive and so far has not transferred to its progeny. In the process of trying to produce the elusive yellow-flowered hybrids, however, some remarkable new hybrids have resulted. Most have the small, trailing foliage and large flowers of *I. repens*, with the flower colors of *I. walleriana*. Some of these will shortly be appearing on the gardening market. In time we may yet see the true yellow-flowered impatiens or even, dare we hope, the blue-flowered one. Hybrids involving the African species *I. irvingii* have also produced some excellent plants, with large star-shaped flowers on plants with a more upright habit than that of *I. irvingii*.

A few hybrids between *I. niamniamensis* and both *I. auricoma* and *I. walleriana* have been produced. Although novel in having new flower shapes and

Impatiens repens
× *I. walleriana* hybrid

Impatiens auricoma
× *I. niamniamensis* hybrid

Impatiens niamniamensis
× *I. walleriana* hybrid

Long-sepaled *Impatiens niamniamensis*
× *I. clavicalcar* hybrid

Black-leaf *Impatiens epiphytica*
× *I. clavicalcar* hybrid

Madagascan hybrid,
Impatiens auricoma
× *I. bicaudata*

colors, sadly they have not been considered commercially viable enough to warrant the huge expense of marketing them.

For the greenhouse gardener, there have been some interesting new crosses made using *Impatiens niamniamensis* and species such as *I. epiphytica* and the yellow-flowered *I. clavicalcar*. The new, as-yet-unnamed hybrids make very colorful pot plants, and some of these are already being offered by a few nurseries.

One very encouraging development with interspecific hybridization was the discovery that certain Madagascan species have the capacity to interbreed, which has led to a great many new and colorful hybrids. The Madagascan caudiform succulent *Impatiens tuberosa* and *I. auricoma*, from the Comoros, had been known to cross for some time, but now other species have been included with good effect. For instance, *I. bicaudata* and *I. bisaccata* have improved the color range even more. All these species and hybrids have rather cup-shaped flowers with short, bifid, incurving spurs. Recently, a species with flat, open-faced flowers and long spurs was found on Madagascar and described as *I. laurentii*, giving scope for a far wider range of hybrid traits. Most of these hybrids are very floriferous and, unlike many other impatiens, they tend to hold their flowers above the foliage. The Madagascan hybrids are particularly strong growers and are far more drought tolerant than the more common garden impatiens. The plants are much larger in size than *I. walleriana* hybrids, but the downside is, like them, they are frost tender, so cuttings should be taken in autumn to overwinter in the greenhouse. Alternatively they can be lifted and potted into large pots to overwinter in a frost-free greenhouse. Some of the Madagascan hybrids have made their way into nursery lists under such names as *I. auricoma* 'Jungle Gold' and *I.* 'Jungle Orange'. In time, they are sure to become very popular additions to the gardens of Europe and the United States.

Many of the annual species from the Himalayas have also shown an ability to interbreed. For instance, *Impatiens balfourii* naturally hybridizes with *I. pseudobicolor*, forming large hybrid colonies. Under cultivated conditions, these Himalayan annuals may be in contact with a wide range of different pollinators, and some have produced hybrids. The progeny are nearly always

Madagascan hybrid, *Impatiens tuberosa* × *I. laurentii*

Madagascan hybrid, *Impatiens tuberosa* × *I. auricoma*

Madagascan hybrid, (*Impatiens auricoma* × *I. bicaudata*) × *I. laurentii*

Madagascan hybrid

sterile and often misshapen, however, bearing little similarity to either of the parents. It is a matter of some debate as to whether the resulting hybrids are of any great improvement on the parent plants.

Impatiens walleriana is generally not so prolific in flowering, but breeders have selected the best clones in color, flowering capacity, and growth habit to offer us the wonderful range we have today. In addition to the natural colors of red, pink, lilac, and white, plants with salmon, orange, and purple flowers have been developed. The first serious breeding of *I. walleriana* was begun in 1956 by Bob Reiman of the Ball Seed Company in the United States, who improved on the rather tall busy Lizzie to create a more compact plant, with a bushier habit and larger flowers. During the 1960s, Claude Hope of the Pan American Seed Company developed a larger range of colors, offering eight distinctly different new colors.

The now-famous Elfin series was introduced to the trade in 1968 by Claude Hope of the Pan American Seed Company—the busy Lizzie, as we know it today, had arrived. Since then, several new ranges have been offered, such as the Accent and Tempo series, which are even more compact than the Elfin plants, and more recently the larger-flowered Bruno impatiens. The range has been improved even further with the addition of bicolored flowers, in the forms of the Starbright, Mosaic, and Picotee series and more recently the Stardust series from Ball Horticultural. Current breeding of *Impatiens walleriana* has been directed toward even smaller, bushier plants that start branching closer the ground, without the need for pinching out the tips, producing even more flowers. The petite Firefly series from Ball Horticultural has much smaller flowers but makes up for this by producing many more of them, completely covering the plant. These are now available in a wide selection of colors.

We have also seen the arrival of the Mini Hawaiian series. These diminutive plants are miniature in every sense, and many have bicolored flowers, streaked and blotched quite unlike any other of their larger-flowered relatives. Originally bred in Japan, some found their way to Hawaii, where they were subjected to further selective breeding and where these color combinations were developed. The Mini Hawaiian and Firefly series are particularly useful for window boxes and patio containers, as a greater number of colors and combinations of colors can be accommodated in quite small spaces.

Impatiens walleriana
'Expo Red Star'
Ball Horticultural

Impatiens walleriana
'Mosaic'
Ball Horticultural

Impatiens walleriana 'Accent'
Ball Horticultural

Impatiens walleriana 'Expo Star Mixed' Ball Horticultural

Impatiens walleriana 'Red'
Ball Horticultural

Impatiens walleriana
'Rose Picotee'
Ball Horticultural

Double-flowered forms, with their miniature rose-like flowers, resulted from a chance mutation in *Impatiens walleriana*. Although they can be grown from seed, a good percentage of them may turn out to be semi-double, so it is worthwhile selecting the better ones and propagating from these. Virtually all double-flowered *Impatiens* are sold as pot plants and are intended for use as container plants or as flowering houseplants, and millions of them are produced yearly to satisfy the demands of the garden center trade. They are propagated by cuttings taken from only the best, virus-free stock plants selected for their color, habit, and uniformity. Double-flowered hybrids are available in a good range of colors, which includes red, salmon, pink, magenta, white, and bicolored. They make good bedding plants, but are at their best grown in pots, where they bloom continuously. Some of the new Dazzler series of bicolors are quite striking.

Impatiens walleriana
'Firefly Red' (Firefly series)
Ball Horticultural

Impatiens walleriana
'Red and White'
(Mini Hawaiian series)

Impatiens walleriana
'Hawaii' (Mini
Hawaiian series)

Red and white *Impatiens walleriana* 'Circus'
Ball Horticultural

Impatiens walleriana 'Pink Fancy'
Ball Horticultural

Impatiens walleriana 'Fiesta Sparkler' red and white
Ball Horticultural

Impatiens walleriana
'Variegata'

Impatiens walleriana
'Balolepep'
(Fiesta series)
Ball Horticultural

In recent years there has been a good deal of interest in variegated forms, both as single- and double-flowered varieties. These are real eye-catchers, with the same flowers but with the addition of green and cream- or white-splashed foliage. The first of these variegated forms was *Impatiens walleriana* 'Variegata' a single-flowered plant with cream and green foliage, sometimes called "patient Susie" because of its reluctance to set seed. It is a very attractive plant with magenta flowers.

Variegation is characterized by the uneven distribution of chlorophyll in one or more of the layers of surface tissues of the leaves. This condition is thought to have two main causes: viral contamination transmitted by aphids or some other leaf-sucking insect, or mutation or sporting. Therefore, variegated forms cannot be propagated by seed, but must be produced from cuttings. Variegation in flowers causes streaking of the pigment and is known to be transmitted virally. The virus seems to have little or no effect on the plant's health and appears to be quite stable. Dutch bulb growers have exploited the disease to create new varieties of tulips, achieved by actively encouraging aphids to spread the virus.

Most of the foliar variegation of *Impatiens* appears to have originated by chance mutation of green-leafed plants developing abnormally blotched and streaked leaves on an otherwise normal side shoot. Because the cells in such a leaf have different genetic compositions, these are often referred to as chimeras, after the Greek mythological beast with a lion's head, a goat's body, and a serpent's tail. When such a shoot is detached and rooted, the variegation in the resultant plant is permanent. Occasionally, a variegated plant may develop the odd leaf that has reverted back to the original green; if left, the plant will revert back to being completely green. Therefore, it is a good idea to remove the green shoots, as they are often more vigorous than the var-

Impatiens
walleriana
'Kingswood'

iegated ones. Impatiens plants have also sported yellow and lime green and even completely yellow leaves. This variegation seems to enrich the colors of the flowers by providing a multicolored backdrop for the flowers to be displayed. The leaves of some impatiens have dark green to maroon coloring, but this is the completely natural state of some species in the wild, and some are even selected for this.

Much recent work on these variegated plants has been carried out in the United States by breeders such as Doug Lohman in Ohio. He has introduced many named varieties, such as

A variegated form of *Impatiens niamniamensis*

Impatiens walleriana 'Kingwood', I. *walleriana* 'Robert Burns', and I. *walleriana* 'Cherry Lemonade'.

Variegation of impatiens is not exclusive to *Impatiens walleriana*. It has also appeared in other species, such as *I. niamniamensis*, also known as the "Congo cockatoo." The larger leaves of this species provide a greater base to display the variegation, which in turn shows off its colorful flowers really well. *Impatiens niamniamensis* 'Golden Cockatoo' appeared as a sport on a plant in the greenhouses of Bourn Brook Nurseries in Essex in 1995. This cultivar was grown on for a while to establish its stability and has since become available worldwide.

4

New Guinea Hybrids

I n recent years the New Guinea hybrids have become extremely popular and now even rival the more common *Impatiens walleriana* cultivars for use in patio planting. Since their introduction in 1972, the New Guinea hybrids have steadily grown in popularity, so much so that many millions of them are produced by nurseries worldwide every year, mainly in the form of rooted cuttings. The plants can produce a wonderful show in large pots, window boxes, and even hanging baskets and can also be used as bedding plants. In early summer garden centers are awash with the color of their blooms, and gardeners find these plants, with their large flowers and showy leaves, quite irresistible. The New Guinea hybrids can flower abundantly all summer through, up to the first frosts. If moved into the greenhouse with a little heat or brought indoors and placed in a well-lit position, such as on a windowsill, they can be overwintered for growing on the following year. The New Guinea hybrids stand up well to wind and rain and are adaptable to most light conditions, from full sun to fairly heavy shade, and they are free from damage caused by most insect pests. These hybrids can be rather thirsty plants, however, originating as they do from species living in the heat and humidity of the steamy rain forests of Papua New Guinea. They have a poor moisture-retention ability; when dry, the plants will start to wilt alarmingly quickly, so care should be taken to see that they are well watered regularly.

The New Guinea species *Impatiens hawkeri* was the first of these to be collected, in Papua New Guinea in 1884 by Lt. Hawker R.N. The plants were sent to the Adelaide Botanical Gardens in Australia, and pressed specimens were sent to the herbarium at Kew. *Impatiens hawkeri* plants were then grown by Dr. Richard Schomburgk in the gardens at Adelaide, and two years later some plants were sent to William Bull, a Chelsea nurseryman, who described the species in his *Catalogue of New, Beautiful and Rare Plants* (1886). *Impatiens hawkeri* was again described more fully in the *Gardeners' Chronicle* of the same year. A more complete description by J. D. Hooker appeared in the *Curtis Botanical Magazine* in April 1909. Over the years, *I. hawkeri* has been cultivated in many botanic gardens and was very popular in the late 19th century as a greenhouse plant. This species is often attacked by the begonia mite (*Tarsonemus* spp.), however, and at one point was nearly lost to cultivation.

After the discovery of *Impatiens hawkeri*, the New Guinea region was searched for new species over the next few decades by German, English, and Dutch botanists. About 15 species were identified, all of which are now regarded as various forms of *I. hawkeri*, although they are sometimes still known by their synonyms: *I. herzogii, I. klossii, I. nivea, I. lauterbach, I. linearifolia, I. mooreana, I. polyphylla, I. rodatzii, I. schlecteri,* and *I. trichura.* All these varieties were found to possess similar characteristics and were able to form hybrids with each other. The resulting plants were fertile, supporting the theory that they were all varieties of the same species. Two true species from neighboring islands, *I. platypetala* from Java and *I. aurantiaca* from Celebes (Sulawesi), also formed hybrids with these varieties, but in these cases the resulting plants were sterile.

In 1970 the U.S. Department of Agriculture in conjunction with the Longwood Gardens Foundation sponsored a plant hunting expedition to New Guinea. They sent H. F. Winters and J. J. Higgins to search specifically for new species of rhododendron, begonia, and ferns. While there, however, Winters and Higgins also found many diverse *Impatiens* plants. With the aid of native helpers, they collected more than 50 specimens for shipment back to the United States. Unfortunately, only 25 of the plants survived the journey back. After a period of quarantine, Longwood Gardens was given cuttings of the original stock and breeding programs were initiated in 1971 and 1972. The first crosses were released in late 1972 for use as bedding plants. In the same year, the U.S. Department of Agriculture released material of the origi-

Micropropagated plants growing in test tubes Fischers

nal New Guinea stock to various botanical gardens, research institutes, and plant breeding stations for further, more extensive work.

The next 25 years saw tremendous progress in the breeding of new and better New Guinea hybrids. The originally collected plants were rather tall and spindly, with little branching. After considerable work by breeders, the trade has produced much more compact plants with good branching and ear-lier and more prolific flowering. Some of these new introductions also have highly variegated leaves in colors of green, yel-low, orange, cream, pink, and red, and others have solid dark green or burgundy red, almost black leaves. The leaf shapes range from broadly elliptical to nar-rowly lanceolate. The flower color range extends from red, orange, magenta, pink, and purple to white, with many bicolored varieties available. A good deal of the success in this breeding can be attributed to the great diversity within the original collected plants. Another recent break-through was the introduction of double-flowered varieties, such as the Suncatcher and Pinwheel series. Although the flowers are not fully double, they do make a wel-come addition, and there is a wide range of colors to choose from.

Mass cultures growing in the laboratory Fischers

The first New Guinea impatiens seed offered in the trade was the orange-flow-ered *Impatiens hawkeri* 'Tango' in 1989, with an improved version released in 1994. The first New Guinea hybrid seed mix was offered by the Pan American Seed Com-pany in 1992, and both these and *I. hawkeri* 'Tango' have since become widely avail-able from seed merchants. These hybrids contain a good range of colors, some with variegated leaves.

Mature plants growing on trial benches

Some plant breeders are now concentrating their work on other aspects, such as drought tolerance and susceptibility to red spider mites (*Tetranychus urticae*). Based on genetic testing, there appears to be a gene in at least one of the original plants that causes a degree of tolerance to drought conditions and a gene in another that gives some immunity from attacks by red spider mites. If this proves to be the case, it may be possible to introduce these qualities into the hybrids through a selective breeding program.

The flowers of the original New Guinea plants were nearly all a single color; although these are still popular, many new bicolored varieties are now available. As with *Impatiens walleriana* hybrids, the quest for the first yellow-flowered New Guinea hybrid has been ongoing for many years. The elusive yellow is the holy grail for New Guinea breeders, and many crosses have been made using yellow-flowered species, such as *I. repens* from Sri Lanka and *I. auricoma* from the Comoros. The gene producing the yellow flowers seems to be recessive, however, and breeders are having difficulty transmitting it into the hybrids. In 2001 the German firm Fischers offered a plant named *Impatiens* 'Vision Yellow', which is an interspecific cross with *I. auricoma* in its genealogy. Although the flower may be described as more of a primrose color, it is undoubtedly a shade of yellow.

One of the attractions of many of the New Guinea species is the leaf coloration, and initially there was a great deal of work carried out in creating varieties with the most colorful leaves. This coloration tends to be seasonal, however, requiring good light and warmth to sustain it. In the cooler conditions of Europe and the northern United States, the colors are not so long lived and the plants tend to revert back to their base colors. Therefore, nurseries began to breed out this feature to produce more uniform plants for garden centers. But now this trend seems to be reversing, and hybrids with colored leaves seem to be back in vogue. Unfortunately, many of the most colorful varieties are a little shy to produce many flowers. Therefore, plant breeders have been evaluating plants that show the best color retention in the leaves in seasons when light levels are not optimum, as well as better flower production. The results have been very promising. Fischers nurseries have produced the Painted Paradise series, which seems to combine the best of both these features.

One of the latest advances in the New Guinea hybrids has been the introduction of double-flowered varieties. These were developed in the 1990s by Ed Mikkelsen at his nurseries in Ashtabula, Ohio, after finding a plant that

Variegated New Guinea hybrid

Impatiens hawkeri 'White' (Painted Paradise series) Innova Plant

Impatiens hawkeri 'Orange Red' (Painted Paradise series) Innova Plant

had produced an extra petal on one of its flowers, although a little small-er than the normal ones. He produced seed from the flower and started a breeding program to try to increase the number of petals per plant. Over the next 10 years Mikkelsen Inc. bred plants giving seven, eight, or nine petals, eventually getting as many as 26 petals. Although Mikkelsen managed to get plants that were considered to be double, it may be fairer to say they are semi-double. These were then released to the trade as the Twice as Nice series.

The double-flowered and variegated *Impatiens hawkeri* 'Salmon Suncatcher' Oglevee

Impatiens hawkeri 'Pinwheel' Oglevee

Impatiens hawkeri 'Blush Pink' (Gem series) Oglevee

    With the rise in popularity of patio planting, there has also been a quest for a more trailing form of impatiens. Ball Horticultural has bred a new strain of these trailing plants called the Fanfare series. Originally only available in purple- and lilac-flowered forms, they are now offered in a much wider

Impatiens hawkeri 'Red' (Gem series)

Impatiens hawkeri 'Blush'
(Fanfare series) Ball Horticultural

Impatiens hawkeri
'Orange'
(Fanfare series)
Ball Horticultural

color range. Although the plants are said to trail, they are now being sold as "spreading impatiens." The flowers are not quite as large as the normal New Guineas hybrids, but they are produced in profusion. Varieties within the Fanfare series are best used as patio container plants or as landscape bedding, but they are a little thirsty, needing watering more frequently than other New Guinea impatiens.

5

Gardening with Impatiens

With their wide tolerance of moisture, soil, and light conditions, impatiens can be used in many of the problem places in gardens, from deep shade to full sun. Although *Impatiens walleriana* has become the best-selling plant in garden centers all over the world, selling by the millions annually, generally gardeners know little or nothing about the wealth of other *Impatiens* species.

The *Impatiens walleriana* cultivars and New Guinea hybrids of today are much more floriferous and are available in a far wider range of growing habits compared to those of even 30 years ago. Much of the emphasis of recent breeding has been improving the range for patio planting, mainly for use as container plants and window boxes, as well as for hanging baskets. Impatiens, however, are equally at home in borders or used in more formal bedding arrangements.

The large nurseries worldwide are continually striving to produce better plants, and they have introduced many new innovations such as double-flowered varieties and trailing forms. Many of these newer plants are a result of interspecific breeding, so we can look forward to seeing even more novel introductions in the near future. In the meantime, the many available impatiens cultivars, with flowers that span the complete spectrum, can be used to really good effect in gardens.

Culture of Impatiens

Although *Impatiens walleriana* and *I. balsamina* are easily raised from seed, in general impatiens seed is difficult to germinate. One reason may be due to the seed being unviable. Some *Impatiens* species are thought to have a short period of viability, which can sometimes be measured in weeks or even days.

Quite often, however, the problem is simply one of seed dormancy. This is particularly the case with annual species. In their natural habitats, annual species often encounter long periods of very cold weather conditions, marking the end of their growing period. These species have developed a state of seed dormancy to protect the embryo from these cold conditions. To accomplish this dormant state, some form of growth inhibitor is produced within the seed and the testa (outer skin), which becomes impervious to moisture. Over the winter months, this is gradually broken down, so that with the advent of spring the seed is ready and able to germinate freely.

In order to grow annual *Impatiens* species, gardeners need to simulate these cold winter conditions. This can be achieved by sowing the seed in pots or trays, covering lightly with perlite, so as not to exclude light, then placing outdoors to contend with the winter conditions. Alternatively, the pot can be put into a plastic bag and placed in the bottom of a refrigerator for about four to six weeks; they should be examined from time to time for signs of germination, after which the pot should be reintroduced to warmer temperatures. Under cultivation, however, most annual species self-sow in great profusion.

The seed of some species, such as the Indian *Impatiens parasitica* and *I. chinensis*, go into a dormancy that coincides with long dry periods, which is then broken by the onset of very wet weather, such as the monsoon. Sometimes slow-germinating species can be helped by stratification, chipping the outer skin of the seed with a sharp knife or rubbing the seed with sandpaper, which allows the moisture to permeate the seed.

The fresh seed of most perennial species from lower elevations, where frost is not a problem (including *Impatiens walleriana*), germinate fairly easily and can be sown in the normal way, remembering not to exclude light. Generally, impatiens prefer a slightly acid soil with a pH of 5.5 to 6.5. After germination has taken place, provide enough light to prevent the seedlings from elongating. After the first true leaves have appeared, transplant them into 75-mm pots filled with a free-draining compost to grow on. To get the best results, use a general 20–20–20 fertilizer or a slow-release resin-coated type. When all risk of frost has passed, harden off the plants before planting out. Many *Impatiens* species can be grown as specimen plants. Although some are naturally bushy by nature, they respond well to periodic pinching out of the growing tips, which encourages bushier plants with more flowers, especially in the early stages.

As an alternative way to grow plants, some seed firms are now offering plant plugs of *Impatiens walleriana* cultivars and New Guinea hybrids. Many of these firms offer a range of rooted cuttings, including doubles, variegated doubles, and the new Seashell and Fusion series hybrids.

Impatiens plants are easily increased from cuttings, which can be taken any time during spring or summer. Ideally the cuttings should be young shoots, about 7.5–10 cm long, and from good, healthy plants. Take the cutting with a clean sharp blade, just below a leaf node, and place it in a pot in a mixture of peat and sharp sand, perlite, or vermiculite, then place the pot in a propagator. Alternatively, cuttings can be placed in a vase of water (a transparent glass one works best), where they should root within a week to 10 days. Once rooted, they should be potted on into a free-draining compost, while first sprinkling some compost over the roots to prevent matting. Once established, the plants should be well fed, as most impatiens species respond to regular feeding. If used as patio container plants, in window boxes, or in hanging baskets, it is a good idea to incorporate some water-retaining gel crystals into the compost.

Many impatiens are at their best grown as container plants, where they are well suited to an open position or they can be equally at home in a shaded one. Impatiens can be perfect subjects for window boxes or hanging baskets. One novel way of growing the *Impatiens walleriana* types is

Cuttings rooting in a glass vase

Impatiens hawkeri 'Celebration', apricot- and white-flowered forms
Ball Horticultural

Impatiens walleriana flower ball

in the shape of a flower ball, made by wiring two hanging baskets together and supporting them by means of a stout post hammered into the ground. Begin by lining the baskets with plastic sheet or moss and cutting several 5-cm diameter holes in the lining. Fill the baskets to the top with a good compost that contains some slow-release fertilizer. Then place a length of plastic tube, such as a piece of 5-cm plastic piping, into the center of one of the baskets in an upright position. Make sure that no compost gets into the pipe and clogs it. Next, from the outside in, insert the young plants through holes cut in the sides of the lining, leaving the top clear. Allow a few days for the plants to become established. The next job is to invert the basket with the tube on top of the other—using a piece of plywood or hardboard to keep the compost in place—so that the bottom of the tube is the top position. After removing the hardboard, the baskets can then be wired together to form a complete ball. The ball can be fixed to a post or hung from a strong support. Water the baskets through the plastic pipe at the top of the ball. An impatiens ball makes an attractive feature for the garden, providing lots of color throughout the summer.

Impatiens for the Herbaceous Border

Impatiens balsamina has had a long history of cultivation and has graced cottage gardens for many centuries. This annual species, which grows wild in many Asian countries, seems to have lost some of its popularity in recent years, and a resurgence of these colorful plants is long overdue. This species is one of the easiest plants to germinate, and its growing requirements are quite minimal. The plants produce a large number of camellia-shaped flowers, ranging in color from bright red, pink, purple, and lilac to white. In the wild *I. balsamina* usually produces single flowers, but most seed offered today is for double-flowered varieties, and the taller varieties have largely given way to the more compact and shorter *I. balsamina* 'Tom Thumb'.

Impatiens tinctoria is a tuberous, perennial species found in Ethiopia, Kenya, Tanzania, Uganda, and Malawi that has already made an impact in borders throughout Europe and the United States. The plant can reach quite large proportions, growing to about 1.5–2 m in height, and is very showy, displaying large trusses of fragrant, white flowers with dark magenta central marking, each 5–6 cm across. The plant flowers over a long period during the summer months and is cut down by the first frosts. It then dies back to its rather large, fleshy tubers, which are similar to those of dahlias. If left

Impatiens tinctoria

undisturbed, the resultant clump can provide quite a spectacular display the following spring. *Impatiens tinctoria* has been available for decades and many nurseries are now offering it, so it should be fairly easy to find.

   Impatiens gomphophylla is another African perennial species with a thick fleshy rootstock. This is a tall, upright, largely unbranched plant of about 1 m in height, displaying dozens of yellowish orange and red flowers held close around the stem, much like lupines or foxgloves. The individual flowers are about 3–4 cm long and pouched, and the display gets even better with age as the number of stems increases. *Impatiens gomphophylla* is quite new to cultivation, although a few nurseries are offering it. I feel sure it is destined to become a garden favorite as it becomes more obtainable.

Impatiens gomphophylla

Impatiens omeiana is a smaller perennial plant found growing on Mt. Emei in Sichuan Province of southern China. It is a slightly tuberous perennial species, which is well worth growing for its foliage alone. The leaves are dark green with a cream-colored herringbone stripe running down the central vein. Its large flowers are an apricot color and deeply pouched, terminating in a slightly spiraled spur. The blooms are produced in a many-flowered raceme. On the downside, *I. omeiana* has a short flowering season, extending only from late summer to autumn. There is also an unnamed variety of *I. omeiana* without the patterning on the leaves. This one has creamy flowers identical in every other respect to those of the parent species and is equally useful as a border subject. Both plants have been available for some time and appear to be quite hardy in most places.

Impatiens arguta is a fairly widespread species throughout the temperate areas of Asia and has been offered by quite a few nurseries in recent years. It is a hardy perennial plant worthy of a place in every border, giving a really good summer-long display of purplish blue flowers, with some yellowish markings in the throat and on the outside spur. The fairly large flowers are deeply pouched, but the petals form a rather flat face and are produced singly along the stems. *Impatiens arguta* is quite a bushy plant, growing to about 50 cm in height; if the growing tips are pinched out, the plant will provide an even better display. Due to its widespread distribution in the wild, there is some regional variation, with some varieties flowering more profusely than others. The white-flowered *I. arguta* var. *alba* is also available, and some people believe it to be even better than the parent species. It is considered to be quite hardy in most places.

Impatiens stenantha is a Himalayan hardy perennial with yellow flowers and attractive dark green leaves. The plant is quite bushy and grows to 25–35 cm tall, producing small racemes of curious yellow and maroon, upturned flowers. *Impatiens scabrida* from the Himalayas and *I. edgeworthii* from northern India and Kashmir are two very reliable hardy garden plants. Both are yellow-flowered, upright plants, growing to about 1 m in height. *Impatiens scabrida* and *I. edgeworthii* are well worth growing because of their long flowering seasons. Quite a few seed firms are offering *I. scabrida* and *I. edgeworthii* seed. Due to problems with viability, the seed can sometimes be difficult to germinate. Once established, however, most species will self-seed themselves very easily. In addition, some nurseries are selling young plants of these species.

Impatiens falcifer is a Himalayan annual with bright yellow open-faced flowers, with some red spotting on the dorsal petals. It is very floriferous and grows to 50 cm in height, but the plant is a little lax in habit and will benefit from some support. Another Himalayan annual is the more widespread *I. racemosa*. Compared to *I. falcifer*, this is a smaller, bushier plant with dark reddish green foliage; it produces racemes of small, bright yellow flowers. Both of these plants can be thoroughly recommended.

Impatiens balfourii is native to western Himalayas, Pakistan, northern India, and Nepal. It is a not-to-be-missed annual species with lovely pink and white, open-faced flowers. This well-branched plant grows to about 40–50 cm in height, with racemes of flowers, each about 3–4 cm across. As with many of the annual species, it readily self-seeds every year. *Impatiens balfourii* has been naturalized in France and is widely grown in the United Kingdom.

Impatiens glandulifera is native to Nepal, and it has become quite troublesome as an escaped garden introduction, now naturalized in many areas of Britain and Europe. This species is still worth growing, however, as it is not difficult to control. The plant can grow to 2 m high and displays large racemes of pink to dark purple flowers. Its close relative *Impatiens candida* has pure white flowers and is even better. Both plants are ideal for a position at the back of the border.

Impatiens namchabarwensis is a newly introduced species from Tibet. This species is striking in that it is the only impatiens to have blue flowers. The plant grows to 50–60 cm in height and carries dozens of flat-faced, ultramarine blue flowers, each with upturned spurs. This species is a tender perennial plant best treated as an annual, as it self-seeds well.

While there are a great many annual and perennial hardy species that can be used in garden borders, dozens more garden-worthy species are only half-hardy, including the African species *Impatiens pseudoviola* and *I. kilimanjari*.

They will be perfectly alright throughout the summer months, but cuttings must be taken in late summer or early autumn to overwinter for planting out in the following spring. Some of these half-hardy species are among the most colorful in the genus.

Impatiens pseudoviola is a very small perennial from eastern Africa. The plant is ideal for a position at the front of the border, where it forms neat cushions of flowers measuring 30–40 cm in diameter. The lilac flowers are about 2–2.5 cm across, each with a little purple marking on the petals. Though frost tender, this species does withstand cold weather conditions a little better than the *I. walleriana* cultivars. *Impatiens kilimanjari* is similar to *I. pseudoviola* in stature and growth. This species, however, produces rather striking red flowers, with four bright yellow spots at the center and purple pollen. These two species, with the addition of naturally occurring white-flowered forms, have been crossed extensively, resulting in numerous hybrids in a wide color range, many of which are available in the trade.

The island of Madagascar has provided us with many horticultural gems in the genus *Impatiens*, many of which are more drought tolerant than other species. The perennial *I. bicaudata* is a rather large plant with pouched, bright red flowers with yellow centers and purple pollen, set off against dark green foliage to make a really attractive show. The rather fleshy stems can grow to 7.5–8 cm in diameter. This species can make a fine specimen plant after a few years, but the plant will have to be grown in a large pot and brought into a frost-protected greenhouse every winter or lifted from the garden, repotted, and brought in the greenhouse. *Impatiens bicaudata* has been bred with a few other Madagascan species to create many colorful hybrids. Some Madagascan hybrids are already available in the trade, including *I. auricoma* 'Jungle Gold'.

Impatiens catatii is a delightful red-flowered perennial species from Madagascar, with dark green foliage arranged in whorls of four to six leaves around the stem. The pouched flowers are displayed in the leaf axils, forming tiers at each node. *Impatiens eriosperma* is another species from Madagascar. It is similar to *I. catatii* in many ways, but its red, pouched flowers are singly placed. Because the plant is bushier than *I. catatii*, however, there are just as many flowers. Although these species are not very widely available, I am sure they are going to be winners.

From the nearby Comoro Islands comes *Impatiens auricoma*, a yellow-flowered species that grows to 75 cm in height. It is similar in habit to *I. bicaudata*, but with much lighter foliage. *Impatiens auricoma* flowers prolifically throughout the season and has proven to be an outstanding plant for both borders and patio planting. This species has been used as a parent plant in the breeding of many hybrids, all of which are worthy of a place in our gardens. The colors range from deep purple and deep red to the palest pink and every shade of yellow and orange. With further breeding work on these plants resulting in more dwarfed forms, they will be challenging the more common *I. walleriana* cultivars for garden space.

Impatiens for Patio Planting

The rise in patio gardening has increased steadily with the growth of garden centers, offering an ever-widening range of plant containers and accessories side by side with an endless choice of plants to use in them. It is not difficult to understand why—containers are easy to use and give excellent displays of color for minimal cost. With the introduction of newer trailing varieties and large- and miniature-flowered cultivars, the more common *Impatiens walleriana* cultivars will always take pride of position, but they are now being joined by new *Impatiens* species and interspecific hybrids that will add a great deal of choice for the gardener.

Breeders of the New Guinea hybrids have been offering plants such as those in the Fanfare series, which are as near to trailing as you could wish. In addition, there are the double-flowered Suncatcher and Gem series, which are available in a wide spectrum of flower colors, and the variegated Painted Paradise series, with very colorful leaves. The Butterfly series includes splendid trailing hybrids from crosses between *Impatiens pseudoviola* and *I. walleriana*, offered in a range of five colors. The flowers are just as numerous and a little larger than those of *I. pseudoviola*, about 2–3 cm across. There are also many cushion-forming hybrids of *I. pseudoviola* crossed with *I. kilimanjari* in many flower color variations, which are sure to become very popular.

Other species with a more upright habit include *Impatiens zombensis* from Malawi and Mozambique, which covers itself with dozens of light purple, star-shaped flowers, each about 2 cm in diameter. When *I. usambarensis*, a red-flowered species from northern

Impatiens auricoma
Ball Horticultural

Tanzania, is crossed with *I. walleriana*, it produces a hybrid with a profusion of orange flowers on a taller plant, just right for the center of a large pot or other container.

Although a little tall for growing in a pot, the yellow-flowered *Impatiens auricoma* from the Comoros can be thoroughly recommended for patio planting. Its hybrids in the Seashell and Fusion series give scope for a much wider splash of color. Some of these hybrids, however, have not turned out to be very color-fast under the wet conditions of some parts of Britain and the United States, particularly the yellow-flowered ones.

Impatiens for the Greenhouse and Conservatory

There is a wealth of *Impatiens* species to tempt the greenhouse gardener looking for something new and interesting. Many of the African and Southeast Asian species can be grown outside, especially in warmer areas, but they fare better under the protection of a greenhouse.

Impatiens niamniamensis is an African species already fairly well known as a greenhouse pot plant. This species is perhaps better known under its more common name of "Congo cockatoo," which aptly describes it, with its red and yellow lower sepal resembling the flamboyantly colored beak of a parrot. There is a variegated leaf form of *I. niamniamensis*, as well as many flower-color variations from pink to dark reddish purple. These normally terrestrial plants are often found growing epiphytically in their natural habitat, usually stilted in growth but producing normal-sized flowers. Many *I. niamniamensis* cultivars are now available in nurseries, but you may have to search for them.

Impatiens clavicalcar is a close relative of *I. niamniamensis* that is endemic to the Democratic Republic of the Congo. Its flowers are yellow with larger white petals. Since *I. clavicalcar* was first collected in the wild, it is now believed to have gone extinct, due mainly to the demands of agriculture. I am glad to say that a few nurseries have this species on their lists, and it has been crossed with *I. epiphytica* to form attractive orange-flowered hybrids, with dark, almost black leaves.

Impatiens epiphytica from eastern Tanzania and *I. keilii* from Burundi, Rwanda, and the Democratic Republic of the Congo are two good epiphytic species that prefer shady growing conditions. They make fine pot plants with flowers of red and yellow, with short, upturned spurs, similar to those of *I. niamniamensis*. In addition, *I. epiphytica* and *I. keilii* make excellent subjects to grow as bark-mounted plants, especially in combination with orchids.

Impatiens repens is a superb species from Sri Lanka. This trailing plant has small, reddish green leaves, and large, yellow flowers. *Impatiens repens* is often found in botanic gardens, used in hanging baskets and growing much like *Columnea*. Another good trailing plant is *Impatiens cordata* from southern India, with small glossy leaves and large, pale lilac flowers, each with two dark purple blotches at the center. *Impatiens cordata* is not as prolific in flowering as the other species, but this species is worth trying.

A few years ago a new plant labeled *Impatiens* 'Velvetea' or *Impatiens* 'Secret Love' appeared on the sales benches of some garden centers and superstores. No one seemed to know anything about it. Was it a new hybrid or a new species? Some said it was a new find from West Africa. After a great deal of research, Christopher Grey-Wilson finally put an end to the speculation. He identified the plant as *Impatiens morsei*, a species found in Guangxi Province in China and first described by J. D. Hooker 150 years ago. In the wild *I. morsei* is quite variable in color, giving reason for the difficulty in its identification. However, it has been grown in the Guangxi Botanical Gardens for some time, which is the probable source of the plant. *Impatiens morsei* is a really beautiful, tender species with dark green, velvety leaves with the

Impatiens sodenii

addition of a striking pinkish magenta midvein. The flowers are quite large, almost inflated, pouched, and white with bright orange and yellow markings in the throat. The plant that eventually entered the horticultural trade was acquired by Marinke de Haas van Dijk as an unidentified species from the Amsterdam University Botanic Gardens, without any collection details. After a great deal of work in breeding and selection, *Impatiens morsei* 'Velvetea' was developed and eventually introduced into the trade. The cultivar was meant to be sold as a houseplant, but it can be grown very easily in the greenhouse, giving some winter protection. Because it is quite succulent, this plant should only be kept moist, as overwatering will quickly cause it to decay.

Impatiens sodenii from Kenya and Tanzania is a rather large plant that is great for the larger greenhouse or conservatory. It has large, glossy, light green leaves arranged in whorls. Its large, flat flowers are variable in color, from pure white to white with magenta markings at the center or lilac with a white eye. When grown in a large pot in the conservatory, *I. sodenii* can make a magnificent display, and with a little winter heat, this plant can remain in flower throughout the year.

Impatiens kinabaluensis, found on Mt. Kinabalu in Borneo, is another good species that has only recently been described. The plant has pink flowers, with large heart-shaped dorsal petals, and it produces many flowers throughout the season.

6

Pests and Diseases

Impatiens are fairly vigorous plants and are not troubled by many insect pests. Unlike most plants, slugs and snails do not present a great problem to them, and although many *Impatiens* species are visited by pollinating butterflies and moths, they are rarely attacked by their caterpillars. Under cultivation, however, there are a few troublesome insects: vine weevils, whiteflies, red spider mites, thrips, mealy bugs, and scale insects. Fungal and viral diseases may also attack impatiens.

Prevention is better than cure, so hygiene is very important and early treatment of affected plants is of paramount importance. Once an offending insect or disease gets a foothold, it becomes difficult to control. There are countless chemical insecticides on the market, but current trends are being centered around the use of biological control, mostly by the use of various natural predators. These predators are specific to the offending pest and are usually not harmful to beneficial insects in the garden. Many firms are now breeding these biological control agents, and you can find them advertised in the gardening press. Before introducing these predators to the garden or greenhouse, it is important that no chemical insecticide residue is left remaining on your plants.

Black vine weevil (*Otiorhynchus sulcatus*)

This insect is one of the most pernicious of pests. It attacks most pot plants, both under glass and outdoors, leaving its telltale notches on the leaf edges. Often this is the first indication that all is not well. These flightless weevils are slow moving, nocturnal creatures that feed on the foliage. The eggs are laid just below the surface of the soil, where they soon hatch as white 1-cm-long grubs. These larvae then start devouring the roots, ultimately burrowing their way into the stem. The otherwise healthy plant suddenly collapses, and it is often not until this point that the gardener notices what has been taking place.

Black vine weevils have become particularly troublesome in Britain and Europe and are getting worse all the time. One of the most effective biological treatments is to drench the whole pot with a solution containing nematodes. These tiny worms attack the weevil grubs, eventually killing them. Unfortunately, the nematodes are only active under warm summer conditions. Recently, the new chemical treatment imidacloprid has come on the market as an additive to potting compost, and it is effective any time of the year. It is in granular form and is dissolved in water, then drenched over the soil of established container-grown plants. It is said to give six months protection. As well as controlling the vine weevil, imidacloprid also controls sciarid flies, whiteflies, and aphids. Care should be taken when using imidacloprid in the garden, however, as studies have shown a possible negative impact on bee populations and an ability to cause eggshell thinning in some songbirds. In addition, imidacloprid can be toxic to plants if not used according to manufacturer's instructions.

Greenhouse whitefly (*Trialeurodes vaporariorum*)

Another pest that has become very troublesome is whitefly, the adults of which are only about 1 mm long. In the past, whiteflies were only found occasionally on greenhouse pot plants, but recently more vigorous strains have appeared that are hardy enough to cause damage to plants growing outside. Under glass the trouble is greater, because the honeydew secreted by whiteflies attracts unsightly black mold.

These new whitefly strains are becoming resistant to most insecticides. Therefore, if treating whiteflies with insecticide, it is best to use a different insecticide each time you treat the plants. Plants should be treated every two weeks; although a single treatment may eliminate the adult flies, their eggs hatch out in a week to 10 days. Biological control for whiteflies is accomplished by using tiny *Encarsia formosa* parasitic wasps. They lay their eggs on the shell cases of the whiteflies; when the wasp larvae hatch, they consume the whitefly. As with other biological control agents, their success depends on sufficiently warm temperatures, and new adult wasps must be reintroduced periodically as the pest populations die off.

Red spider mite (*Tetranychus urticae*)

Contrary to its common name, this pest is not a spider, nor is it red. The red spider mite is actually a rather tiny, light brown to green, sap-sucking mite, barely visible to the naked eye. It is most prevalent under warm, dry conditions and can often be found on the under surface of leaves. Bad infestations show heavily spotted patterning on the upper leaf surface and a tracery of tiny cobwebs on the undersides.

Red spider mites are difficult to control due to the fact that they have become resistant to many of the more common pesticides. Providing cooler, damper conditions can be helpful, and spraying plants with solutions of insecticidal soft soap can keep them down. The more effective chemical treatments contain bifenthren which should be used three times at seven-day intervals. Biological treatment uses the predatory mite *Phytoseiulus persimilis*, which consumes adult red spider mites as well as the eggs. To become active, this predator needs temperatures of 21°C (70°F) and good light.

Thrips (*Frankliniella occidentalis*)

Thrips are tiny, winged, sap-sucking insects and are among the worst of all greenhouse pests. Thrips have the capacity to breed very quickly at any time of the year. The entire life cycle from egg to adult lasts only 10 days, so infestation takes only a short time. Thrips are light brown and have the ability to fly from plant to plant with ease. Like whiteflies, thrips do their damage on the undersides of the foliage, often before it is noticed, unless plants are regularly inspected. The eggs develop into tiny cream-colored larvae that do just as much damage as the adults. Once a larva has fed on a virus-infected plant, it can spread the disease to other plants for the duration of its life.

Thrips relish dry, warm conditions, so keeping plants well watered and regularly sprayed can help, as can damping down staging and floors. Chemical control is in the form of insecticidal sprays containing bifenthren or imidacloprid. Biological control can be attained through the use of predatory mites, which can be obtained from mail order firms specializing in these treatments.

Mealy bugs (*Planococcus citri*)

These are tiny, waxy-coated, fleshy, segmented insects that resemble tiny woodlice. The mature female is about 5 mm long and usually found at the upper parts of the plant, in leaf joints. Mealy bugs are sap-sucking insects that secrete large amounts of honeydew, which fosters the development of black sooty mold that may cover the foliage.

A paintbrush dipped into methylated spirits and applied to the pest will usually kill it by dissolving the waxy protective covering. Insecticides containing the toxin imidacloprid, used as a systemic spray, can provide protection lasting for a few weeks.

Scale insects (*Pulvinaria* species, *Diaspis* species)

There are more than 25 species of scale insects in the United Kingdom alone, and scales may attack plants grown both inside the greenhouse as well as outside. Scales are sap-sucking insects that derive their name from the shell-like waxy covering that conceals their bodies. They look like tiny brown blisters on the stems and leaves of plants. Scale insects attach themselves to stems and leaves and are stationary for most of their lives; only in the very early life stages do they quickly move from plant to plant. Their sap feeding may cause yellowing or wilting of leaves, stunted plant growth, or even death when the infestations are very heavy.

Small parasitic wasps and predatory lady beetles can be used to significantly reduce scale insect populations. Removing scale insects by hand may be practical for light infestations, and heavily infested stems can be pruned out. Dormant oils can be sprayed on plants prior to bud break, and insecticidal soaps may prove effective. Insecticides containing the toxin imidacloprid can be effective remedies.

Fungal diseases

Most fungal diseases can be kept under control by practicing good sanitation, namely picking off dead leaves and flowers and disposing of them. Good ventilation in the greenhouse or conservatory and the use of compost with good drainage for pot plants will also help to control fungus. There are many fungicidal preparations on the market that can be helpful, such as copper sulfate pentahydrate. Care should be taken when applying this compound, however, as this chemical is harmful or fatal if swallowed, and it can cause irritation of the eyes, skin, and respiratory tract.

Viral diseases

The two main viruses that affect *Impatiens* are impatiens necrotic spot virus and tomato spotted wilt virus. The symptoms are the appearance of black ring spots, mosaics, and necrotic spots, with brown or tan colored markings. Flowers can appear to be streaked, and leaves become distorted and yellowed. Stems sometimes develop black areas or lesions, and the plants appear stunted. Control is focused on prevention, as there is no cure available. Once a plant is infected, it must be removed and disposed of to prevent cross-contamination.

7

Impatiens of Africa

The African continent is a great storehouse of botanical treasures, and the genus *Impatiens* figures quite prominently among the countless riches to be found there. To date, well over 100 African species have been described, and doubtless many more are still waiting to be discovered. Of course, the best known of these is *I. walleriana*, which has for many years remained atop the list of summer bedding plants, due to the numerous cultivars available. Some of the other African species are beginning to make their presence felt to the gardening public as well.

Impatiens tinctoria is one that has been steadily gaining in popularity, and nurseries have been offering it for some years. It is a tall, tuberous species found in Kenya, Uganda, and Malawi. Because it grows to 2 m high, this species is ideal for a position in the back of the border. *Impatiens tinctoria* has large white flowers, with magenta purple central markings. It is reasonably hardy in warmer regions, but may need some winter protection in other areas. If left undisturbed for a few years, *I. tinctoria* will form a large clump and provide a really showy display. *Impatiens flanaganae* is a close relative found in South Africa. This species is also tuberous and similar to *I. tinctoria* in many other respects, but *I. flanaganae* produces rosy pink flowers and is a little shorter in stature. Both species are herbaceous perennials that die back to the tubers during the dry season in their native habitat, emerging again during the rainy season. In Europe and the United States, this dieback coincides with our winter, very much like dahlias. Although not dependably hardy in all parts of Britain and the United States, with the protection of straw mulch, *I. tinctoria* and *I. flanaganae* should come through the winter alright.

For the front of the border, there are a few African species that can put on a good show. *Impatiens pseudoviola*, native to Tanzania, is a plant that makes a neat cushion of small lavender flowers, no more than 10–15 cm high and 20–30 cm across. There is also a white-flowered variety, *I. pseudoviola* 'Alba', with the same neat habit. The flowers of this species are not very large, but the plant makes up for that by flowering profusely throughout the summer. Both are now freely available as nursery-grown plants, and some magenta- and red-flowered hybrids are also being offered. Although *I. pseudoviola* is not frost hardy, it will fare better than *I. walleriana* at lower temperatures.

Quite a few African species would make fine additions to the patio as container plants. For instance, *Impatiens zombensis* is one well worth trying. It makes a bushy plant, about 30–40 cm high, and is covered in small, purple, star-shaped flowers all summer long. *Impatiens zombensis* can be grown easily from seed obtained from specialist seed firms. Another worthwhile species is *I. usambarensis*, from northern Tanzania. It has large, flat, red *I. walleriana*–type flowers on a more erect and taller plant. Crosses between *I. usambarensis* and *I. walleriana* have produced hybrids with orange-red flowers and a much bushier habit. Both of these species make excellent garden plants, and are particularly well suited to larger containers.

Impatiens kilimanjari is a colorful species that comes from the southern slopes of Mt. Kilimanjaro in Kenya. Its small, bright red, star-shaped flowers have the unusual attraction of four yellow spots on the lateral petals, complimented with a yellow spur. It is a trailing species that roots at the nodes where it touches the ground, making *I. kilimanjari* ideal for the patio.

Impatiens hoehnelii, also from Kenya, is another trailing plant with good possibilities. This species has light purple, flat, butterfly-shaped flowers, 3 cm across, borne along thin stems that take root wherever they touch the soil. The plant's unusually shaped flowers stand out from the quite small leaves, and it can be highly recommended for use as a hanging basket or patio container plant.

Impatiens gomphophylla is a slightly tuberous species native to southern Tanzania, Zambia, and Malawi. It has recently come into the horticultural trade, and is one I am sure we shall be seeing a lot more of in the future. It is an upright plant, growing to about 1 m in height and carrying a profusion of orange-red and yellow flowers grouped closely to the stems. *Impatiens gomphophylla* can be grown as a hardy perennial in some parts of Britain and the United States, but it is probably best treated as half-hardy in most areas.

The Species

Impatiens apiculata De Wildeman

One of a group of species including *I. stuhlmannii, I. masisiensis, I. apiculata,* and *I. warburgiana,* all very similar in growth habit, flower shape, and size. *Impatiens apiculata* is a straggling, branched species growing to about 1 m long, rooting at the nodes where they touch the ground. Leaves usually spiraled, although opposite and occasionally even whorled arrangements can be found on the same stem. Leaves 10 cm by 5 cm, ovate, crenate edges. Flowers single or in umbels of two or three blooms, large, 4.5 cm wide, bright pink. Seed capsule spindle-shaped. *Impatiens apiculata* is found growing in the Democratic Republic of the Congo, Uganda, and Rwanda. It has been offered by some nurseries in Britain.

Impatiens assurgens Baker f.

Erect, perennial species growing to 80 cm tall, simple, with few branches, rising from a crown above fleshy roots, varying from glabrous to pubescent. Leaves oppositely arranged, often crowded near the top of the stem, sessile, or with very short petioles, oblong-ovate or elliptical, margins shallowly serrate-dentate. Flowers white or pale pink, sometimes with orange yellow spots near the center, solitary or in axillary fascicles of two or three; lateral sepals ovate-lanceolate, lower sepal 1 cm long, abruptly constricted into 3- to 10-mm long, slightly curved spur; dorsal petal 10 mm by 7 mm, hooded, with narrow dorsal crest, pointed at top; lateral united petals 15–28 mm long, upper pair oblong, smaller than lower pair. Seed capsule fusiform, 1–1.5 cm long. *Impatiens assurgens* is a fairly widespread species found in the Democratic Republic of the Congo, Burundi, Tanzania, Zambia, Mozambique, and Malawi. It is quite a variable plant in every respect, and it favors an open grassland situation.

Impatiens austrotanzanica Grey-Wilson

Erect to slightly decumbent, perennial species, growing to about 1 m in height, sparsely branched, finely pubescent, becoming glabrous. Leaves arranged alternately, 3–13 cm long by 2.5 cm wide, petioled, ovate-elliptical, margins shallowly crenate. Flowers deep red with white or cream anthers and yellow marking in center, occasionally pink or white flowers are found, solitary or in fascicles of two to four; lateral sepals ovate 12 mm long, lower sepal 1–2 cm long, narrowly bucciniform, gradually tapering into an incurving spur, 22–40 mm long, slightly swollen at the tip; dorsal petal 1–1.5 cm across, hooded, with narrow dorsal crest, pointed at top; lateral united petals 10–17 mm long, upper pair larger than the lower. Seed capsule fusiform, 2 cm long. *Impatiens austrotanzanica* is found in southern Tanzania and northern Malawi, growing in shady forests.

Impatiens bequaertii De Wildeman

Lax, weakly stemmed, decumbent, perennial species, growing to about 20 cm in length, rooting where it touches the ground. Leaves arranged alternately, glabrous, dark olive green, 2–4.5 cm long by 1–2.5 cm wide, ovate with pointed or acuminate apex, margins crenate-serrate. Flowers white, sometimes light pink, small, in racemes of three or four; lateral sepals linear-lanceolate, 2 mm long, lower sepal 2–4 cm long, abruptly constricted into a curved, thin spur, 7–9 mm long; dorsal petal 4 mm by 3 mm, slightly hooded; lateral united petals 7–8 mm long, upper pair narrowly oblong, upward curving, lower pair larger, semi-elliptical. Seed capsule fusiform. *Impatiens bequaertii* is found in Rwanda, the eastern part of the Democratic Republic of the Congo, and Uganda. It is a pretty little plant with small flowers and darkish leaves, which may be a candidate for hanging baskets or pots.

Impatiens bicolor Hooker f.

This species is very similar to *I. niamniamensis* and has been grouped with it, but some botanists still prefer to use its original name, deeming *I. bicolor* sufficiently different as to warrant separate species status. Erect perennial species with thick, succulent stems, rather densely leaved, sometimes getting woody and losing lower leaves when conditions are not favorable. Leaves arranged spirally, petioles 1–7 cm long, often with fimbriae near the base. Leaves 6–20 cm long by 4–8 cm wide, broadly ovate-oblong or elliptical, leaf margins crenate, crenations overlapping. Flowers dark purple with white or greenish white petals. In all other respects almost identical to *I. niamniamensis*. *Impatiens bicolor* is found in the Democratic Republic of the Congo and the offshore island of Fernando Po.

Impatiens burtonii Hooker f.

A prostrate to trailing species, rooting at the nodes where it touches the ground, growing to over 1 m in length. Leaves arranged spirally, glabrous, edges crenulate, petioles 3 cm long, ovate to oblong-ovate, 5–7 cm long by 3–5 cm wide, finely pubescent. Flowers pink to white, with yellow central markings, single or in groups of three, 4 cm across, spur 2.5 cm long. Seed capsule fusiform. *Impatiens burtonii* is a very widespread species, found across central Africa from Cameroon, the Democratic Republic of the Congo, Rwanda, and through to Tanzania. This is another species that may be a candidate for use in hanging baskets.

Impatiens cecili N. E. Brown

Thin-stemmed perennial herb growing to 50 cm high, moderately branched, semi-erect, often rooting at the lower nodes, stems sometimes pinkish red. Leaves arranged spirally, 6 cm long by 4 cm wide, ovate to elliptical, edges serrulate to almost denticulate with few fimbriae near the base, petioles, shortly petiolate to sessile. Flowers in axillary position, in fascicles of two or three, occasionally single, pale pink; lateral sepals two, lower sepal 3 cm long, abruptly constricted into a 3-cm curved, filiform spur, small dorsal petal, cupped, lateral petals 2 cm long, upper pair small, triangular, coming to a thin point, lower petal much larger, almost elliptical. Seed capsule fusiform. *Impatiens cecili* is only found in Mozambique and eastern Zimbabwe.

Impatiens cinnabarina Grey-Wilson

Erect perennial species with a fleshy rootstock of long tapering tubers, 1–1.5 cm in diameter, growing to 50 cm in height, moderately branched. Leaves arranged spirally, broadly ovate to suborbicular, leaf margins shallowly crenate-serrate, petioles 2–5 cm long with a few linear glands. Flowers in an inflorescence of two to five blooms at the top of the stem, 4 cm wide, open-faced, orange red with a small purple blotch at the center. Seed capsule fusiform, 2 cm long. *Impatiens cinnabarina* is found in the Uluguru Mountains in eastern Tanzania.

Impatiens clavicalcar E. Fischer

A very similar species to *I. niamniamensis* and a close relative, but having more glabrous or glossy leaves. A thick-stemmed, succulent plant, with bright yellow flowers in fascicles of two to six flowers, sometimes produced directly on the stem; lateral sepals 3–4 mm long, reflexed; dorsal petal and lateral

Impatiens clavicalcar

petals are white, both somewhat larger than in *I. niamniamensis*, 2–2.5 cm long. Lower sepal 2.5–3 cm long. Seed capsule 2 cm long, fusiform. *Impatiens clavicalcar* is a rather beautiful species only found growing in the Democratic Republic of the Congo.

Impatiens columbaria J. J. Bos

A perennial succulent plant, erect, becoming prostrate and rooting at the nodes, stems succulent to 1 cm in diameter, pale maroon or green tinged with red, densely covered in colorless hairs, growing to 30–40 cm long. Leaves arranged spirally, densely pubescent with colorless hairs, deciduous in the dry season, petiole whitish green, lamina 4–8 cm long by 2.5–6.5 cm wide, ovate orbicular, bright green above, lighter green below, veins prominent below, margins crenate, crenatures tipped with fimbriae, except for the lower, where they are replaced by longer red to white fimbriae up to 1 cm long, some held vertical to the leaf surface. Inflorescence racemose, peduncles axillary, 10–15 cm long, erect, tinged with red, flowers four to 10 or more, glabrous throughout, reddish purple; lateral sepals ovate, 3.5 mm long by 2.5 mm wide, lower sepal navicular, 10 mm long by 7.5 mm deep, abruptly narrowing to a paler colored white-tipped spur; dorsal petal 8 mm

Impatiens confusa

by 9 mm, broadly ovate but shallowly cucullate, with shallow crest, lateral petals 17–19 mm long, upper 5–6 mm by 4 mm wide obliquely elliptical, lower petal 13 mm long by 7.5 mm wide, almost triangular, distally elongated. Seed capsule unknown. *Impatiens columbaria* is only found in western Gabon.

Impatiens confusa Grey-Wilson

A sparsely branched perennial species, erect to decumbent, rooting at the lower nodes, glabrous, growing to 1 m high. Leaves arranged in verticils of three or four, petiole 2–5 cm long with a few stipitate glands at the top, just below leaf, leaf 5–10 cm long, broadly ovate to ovate elliptical, margins shallowly crenate. Flowers solitary, open faced, epedunculate, lavender with two small magenta spots at the base of the lateral petals; lateral sepals 4–7 mm long, lanceolate, oblong, lower sepal 1 cm wide by 3.5–4 cm long shallowly navicular, abruptly constricted into a 3.5- to 5-cm long, curved, filiform spur; dorsal petal 1.5 cm by 2 cm, obcordate, with narrow dorsal crest, terminating with an acute point, lateral petals 3 cm across, upper petal 1.5 cm by 1 cm, oblong oval, lower petal 1 cm by 0.9 cm. Seed capsule fusiform, 1.5 cm long. *Impatiens confusa* is only found in southern Tanzania.

Impatiens congolensis G. M. Schultze & Wilczek

Perennial species, 30–60 cm tall, stems simple to weakly branched, often becoming leafless below, finely pubescent, becoming glabrous. Leaves arranged spirally, petiole 2–7.5 cm long, slender, usually with a few fimbriae, leaf lamina 4–15 cm long by 2–5 cm wide, ovate-lanceolate to elliptical, finely pubescent above and below, margins crenate-dentate, the teeth spaced 3–5 mm apart. Flowers axillary, epedunculate, single or in fascicles of two to four, red with yellowish green or bright yellow lower sepal and spur; dorsal petal often pale green, pedicels 1.6–4 cm long; lateral sepals 2–2.5 mm long, lanceolate, lower sepal 9–12 mm long by 18–23 mm deep, saccate, abruptly constricted toward the end and sharply incurved into a 4- to 6-mm spur, finely pubescent; lateral united petals 9–11 mm long. Seed capsule 1.5 cm long, filiform. *Impatiens congolensis* is only found in the Democratic Republic of the Congo, growing in dense rain forest. This species can often be found growing epiphytically.

Impatiens cribbii
Christopher
Grey-Wilson

Impatiens cribbii (Grey-Wilson) Grey-Wilson

This species was previously classified as a subspecies of *I. gomphophylla*, which it resembles. Grows to over 1 m in height, upright, sparsely branched. Leaves alternate, narrowly elliptical-oblong, 6–13 cm long by 1–2.5 cm wide, shortly petioled or sessile, glabrous or with a few hairs. Flowers bright orange red, saccate, with small incurving spur; lateral sepals small and ovate, lower sepal broadly saccate, 10–16 mm long; dorsal petal 1.4 cm by 1 cm, hooded, with shallow dorsal crest; lateral united petals 5–15 mm long, upper and lower obliquely ovate. Seed capsule spindle-shaped, 2 cm long. *Impatiens cribbii* is only found in southern Tanzania, often growing in damp, open grassland. This species would make an excellent garden perennial.

Impatiens digitata Warburg

Scrambling, slightly erect perennial species, rooting at the nodes, new growth densely pubescent,

*Impatiens
digitata*

growing to 50 cm long. Leaves arranged spirally, pilose, leaf margins crenate, 2–6 cm long by 1–2.5 cm wide. Flowers single or in pairs, orange red,
2.5 cm long, lower sepal narrowly pouched, gradually tapering into a green,
slightly incurving spur, the end of which splits into four to six short, finger-
like lobes. Seed capsule fusiform. Three separate subspecies are known, each
found in different mountain ranges. *Impatiens digitata* is only found in northern Tanzania.

Impatiens epiphytica G. M. Schulze

A perennial epiphytic species, sometimes found growing terrestrially, poorly
branched, fairly lax in habit, often rooting at the lower nodes, growing to
30–40 cm higwh. Leaves arranged spirally, 3.5–9 cm long by 1.5–4 cm wide,
ovate-elliptical, margins shallowly crenate, petiolate, petioles 2–6 cm long
with a few fimbriae toward the top. Flowers red and yellow, single or in pairs;
lateral sepals small lanceolate-ovate, lower sepal deeply pouched, red and
yellow, with incurving spur; dorsal petal hooded; lateral united petals small.
Seed capsule fusiform. *Impatiens epiphytica* is found in eastern Tanzania. This
species has been offered by a few nurseries for some time, and it adapts well
to pot culture.

Impatiens etindensis Cheek & E. Fischer

Epiphytic, tuberous, glabrous perennial plant, the spherical-ellipsoid tubers 5–6 cm diameter, growing in the moss and debris on tree branches, each bearing one to several stems, and growing to 20–60 cm long, lax to erect, succulent. Leaves arranged alternately, petioles 1–3 cm long, with 1-mm fimbriae, 8–13 cm long by 2–4 cm wide, margins very shallowly crenate. Flowers vivid red, with yellow margins on dorsal and lateral petals, in one- or two-flowered axillary racemes; lateral sepals two, large, held at 45° from the vertical, toward the stem revealing the spur, obovate, 1.5–1.8 cm long, margins with one or two coarse teeth on each side, lower sepal 8–11 mm long by 1–1.5 cm deep, narrowly saccate, abruptly constricted into thin spur, terminating into an upturned erect, swollen apex; dorsal petal 10 mm by 6 mm, deeply hooded; lateral united petals, 1.2 cm long, upper pair 6.9 mm by 7 mm. Seed capsule unknown. *Impatiens etindensis* is a rare species only found on Mt. Etinde in Cameroon.

Impatiens fischeri Warburg

Another tuberous rooted perennial species, growing to over 1 m high, thinly stemmed, weakly branched. Leaves arranged spirally, 5–10 cm long by 3–6 cm wide, ovate to broadly elliptical, leaf margins crenate-dentate or crenulated, petiole 2–4 cm long, with one to three pairs of rounded petiolar glands near the top. Flowers in racemes of two to five, dark red, two pairs of lateral sepals, lower sepal 1–1.5 cm long, pouched or bucciniform, gradually tapering into a 3- to 4-cm long incurving spur with a slightly swollen tip; dorsal petal cupped, 1 cm by 0.7 cm; lateral united petals 1.8 cm long, upper pair half the size of the lower pair. Seed capsule fusiform, 1.5–2 cm long. *Impatiens fischeri* is only found in the Aberdare Mountains in central Kenya.

Impatiens flammea Gilg

Perennial species, growing to 40 cm or more in height, stems arising from a tuberous rootstock. Stems 2–4 mm in diameter, erect, simple or with few branches, lower fleshy, pale green, glabrous. Leaves arranged spirally, pale green, 3–10 cm long by 3–6 cm wide, broadly ovate to elliptical, margins coarsely crenate to crenate-dentate, petioles 3–6 cm long. Flowers axillary, single or in fascicles of two to three bright orange red, the lower sepal and

spur often deep red, pedicels 3–9 cm long, slender; lateral sepals 5–10 mm long, narrowly falcate, lower sepal 7–13 mm long by 14–20 mm deep, saccate, laterally compressed, abruptly constricted into an incurved filiform spur, 8–18 mm long. Dorsal petal 10 mm by 10 mm, cucullate, with broad crest, terminating in a short point; lateral united petals 7–10 mm long. Seed capsule unknown. *Impatiens flammea* is rare and is only known to grow in southern Tanzania.

Impatiens flammea
Christopher
Grey-Wilson

Impatiens flanaganae Hemsley

Another tuberous rooted species similar in many respects to *I. tinctoria*, how-ever, this plant is a little shorter, growing to 1.5 m tall. Flesh of tubers deep red. Flowers in racemes of three to seven, unspotted pink blooms. The lower sepal is wider than in *I. tinctoria* and the spur shorter, 3–4 cm long. The leaves

Impatiens flanaganae

are similar, about 5 cm by 10 cm, arranged spirally, margins shallowly serrate. *Impatiens flanaganae* has a more restricted distribution than that of *I. tinctoria*, being found only in the Natal region of South Africa, where it is rare and endangered. This species is another really good plant for the herbaceous border.

Impatiens frithii Cheek & L. Csisa

Epiphytic perennial species, growing to 15–20 cm tall, glabrous, stem terete or triangular, flexuous, prostrate, only the upper portion of the stem erect, rooting at the nodes, unbranched, or rarely with shoots arising from stem base. Leaves arranged alternately, 7–13 cm long by 3–5 cm wide, ovate or ovate-elliptical, leaf margins crenate-serrate, teeth separated by an erect hair 1–1.5 mm long, basal pair much longer, 2–9 mm long, top surface dark green, undersides pale green, petioles 2–3 cm long. Flowers bright orange red, with yellow on the lateral petals, in axillary racemes of one to four; two lateral sepals deep red, ovate, 5 mm long, lower sepal narrowly bucciniform, 3–3.5 cm long, including abruptly upturned spur; dorsal petal orbicular, 8–9 mm in diameter, deeply hooded; lateral united petals 8–12 mm long, upper pair twice the size of the lower pair, both elliptical. Seed capsule fusiform. *Impatiens frithii* is only found in Cameroon on Mt. Bacossi and Mt. Etinde.

Impatiens gomphophylla Baker f.

An upright, tall, weakly branched perennial species, growing to 1.5 m high. Leaves shortly petioled or sometimes sessile, narrowly ovate to lanceolate, slightly pubescent, with crenulated to serrate edges. Flowers in groups of two to four, on short peduncles the entire length of the stem. The color is quite variable from yellow to orange and red, often bicolored, about 3–4 cm long, pouched, with a short, incurved spur. Seed capsule spindle-shaped. *Impatiens gomphophylla* is fairly widespread throughout the Democratic Republic of the Congo, Tanzania, Zambia, and Malawi, growing in fairly open grassland. A fine perennial species for the middle of the border, especially once established, and reasonably hardy in most places. *Impatiens gomphophylla* is destined to become very popular with gardeners everywhere, and some nurseries are now beginning to offer it.

Impatiens hians Hooker f.

A thin-stemmed, decumbent, perennial herb, growing to 30–50 cm long, rooting at the nodes, moderately branched. Leaves arranged spirally, petiolate, petioles 1–5 cm long, slender, leaf 4–13 cm long by 3–6 cm wide, ovate to oblong-elliptical or oblong-lanceolate, shallowly crenate, sometimes with a few 3–6 mm long fimbriae near the base. Flowers three to six in racemes in the axils of leaves, dark red to orange red and green, lower sepal 2 cm wide by 3–4 cm long, deeply bucciniform, gradually tapering, abruptly constricted into a 6- to 8-mm long strongly incurved spur; dorsal petal 2 cm by 1 cm, cucullate, with narrow crest; lateral united petals 2–2.5 cm long by 2–3 mm wide. Seed capsule fusiform, 2–3 cm long. *Impatiens hians* is found only in West Africa, Cameroon, and Gabon.

Impatiens hochstetteri Warburg

An erect to procumbent annual species growing to 50 cm long, rooting at the nodes. Leaves arranged spirally with slender petioles 1–5 cm long, ovate to ovate-lanceolate, 2.5 cm long by 1 cm wide, margins crenate to dentate. Flowers small, single in leaf axils, sometimes in pairs, white, pale pink to light mauve, often with a pair of yellow spots at the base of the lower lateral petals. Seed capsule spindle-shaped. *Impatiens hochstetteri* is the most widespread species in Africa, being found in eastern Democratic Republic of the Congo, Sudan, Ethiopia, Uganda, Kenya, Tanzania, Malawi, Angola, South Africa, and Swaziland.

Impatiens hoehnelii T. C. E. Fries

Thinly stemmed, trailing species rooting at the nodes, growing to 30 cm long. Leaves quite small, 3 cm by 4 cm, ovate, with serrated edges. Flowers pale purple, butterfly-shaped, 3–4 cm across, with a 3-cm spur. *Impatiens hoehnelii* is native to Kenya. Because of its trailing habit, this species should be good in hanging baskets.

Impatiens irangiensis E. Fischer

Another epiphytic perennial species, moderately branched, glabrous, thick and succulent, often rooting at the lower nodes, sometimes stem rooting near the base, rather upright growing to 10–50 cm high. Leaves arranged spirally, 14–19 cm long by 4.5–6 cm wide, concentrated near the top of the plant, lanceolate, edges acutely serrate. Flowers single or in pairs, in leaf axils, lower sepal and

Impatiens irangiensis   *Impatiens irvingii*

spur pale green, petals greenish to white; lateral sepals 2–3 mm long, ovate-lanceolate, reflexed, lower sepal and spur 11 mm long by 19–20 mm deep, saccate, spur obtusely tipped, 5–7 mm long; dorsal petal cucullate, 9 mm by 5 mm; lateral united petals 12–13 mm long, upper petal double the size of the lower one. Seed capsule 1.3 mm long, glabrous, fusiform. *Impatiens irangiensis* is only found in the Democratic Republic of the Congo and Rwanda.

Impatiens irvingii Hooker f.

A lax to erect perennial species, branched, growing to 60–70 cm long, fairly succulent stems, often reddish tinged, pubescent. Leaves arranged spirally, short petioles or sessile, 4–12 cm long by 1–4 cm wide, lanceolate to ovate-lanceolate, very pubescent in young growth, dark green on top surface, grayish green on under surface, leaf margins serrate-dentate to serrulate. Flowers flat, *I. walleriana*–shaped, produced in leaf axils, solitary or in groups of two or three, violet to pale purple, with a small white blotch in the throat, approximately 4 cm across, upper and lower petals equal in length, lower sepal white, abruptly constricted into a long filiform spur, 5 cm long. Seed capsule fusiform. *Impatiens irvingii* is a very widespread species found throughout central Africa, from Tanzania in the east to Cameroon in the west and every country in between.

Impatiens keilii Gilg

An epiphytic, occasionally terrestrial, perennial species, succulent pale green stems, with few branches, erect to slightly lax, rooting at the nodes. Leaves arranged spirally, 3.5–7.5 cm long by 1–1.5 cm wide, oblanceolate, shallowly crenate, petiolate, petioles 2–6 cm long with a few fimbriae near the top. Flowers solitary or in pairs, epedunculate, lower sepal deeply pouched, red with a little yellow near the top, lateral petals green; lateral sepals 1.5–2.5 mm long, linear, reflexed, lower sepal 1 cm wide by 2.5 cm long, saccate, abruptly constricted into an incurving, slightly twisted spur; dorsal petal 1 cm by 0.7 cm, hooded, lateral petals 1 cm long, upper larger than the lower. Seed capsule fusiform, 1 cm long. *Impatiens keilii* is found in Burundi, Rwanda, and the eastern part of the Democratic Republic of the Congo.

Impatiens kilimanjari Oliver

Short, straggling, almost trailing perennial plant growing to 30–40 cm long, branched, rooting at the lower nodes. Leaves arranged in verticils of three to five, small, 2.5 cm long by 1.5–2.5 cm wide, margins crenate-denticulate, thin petioles 1–3.5 cm long, usually ovate or crenate to dentate. Flowers single, bright red, 3 cm long, lateral petals with four yellow spots on the lower pair, spur 2.5 cm long, yellow. Seed capsule narrowly spindle-shaped. *Impatiens kilimanjari* is only found in Tanzania on the southern slopes of Mt. Kilimanjaro.

Impatiens keilii

Impatiens kilimanjari

This attractive cushion-forming species makes a good addition to the front of a border.

Impatiens kilimanjari subsp. *poccii* is found on the northern slopes of Mt. Kilimanjaro, differing in being slightly smaller and without the yellow spots. Both the species and this subspecies form hybrids with *I. pseudoviola*.

Impatiens mackeyana Hooker f.

Erect, glabrous species, growing to about 1 m tall. Leaves arranged alternately, 6–18 cm long by 2–9 cm wide, narrowly elliptical to ovate, margins serrate-crenate. Flowers rose to deep purple, solitary or occasionally in pairs; lateral sepals small, ovate, pointed, often with deep serrations on one side, lower sepal 2–5 cm long, saccate, abruptly constricted into a short, incurving spur, 8 mm long; dorsal petal almost orbicular, 1.5 cm, hooded; lateral united petals 2.5–5 cm long, upper pair half the size of the lower pair, broadly elliptical, lower pair 2–4 cm long, almost orbicular. Seed capsule fusiform, 2 cm long. *Impatiens mackeyana* is only found in western Cameroon.

Three distinct subspecies are known. *Impatiens mackeyana* subsp. *mackeyana* Grey-Wilson: leaves lanceolate to narrowly elliptical, glabrous, 6–18 cm long by 2–3 cm wide. Found in eastern Nigeria and southwestern Cameroon. *Impatiens mackeyana* subsp. *zenkerii* Grey-Wilson: leaves broadly elliptical, usually with slight indentation near base, 5–18 cm long by 3–8 cm wide; lateral sepals with one to four acute teeth along one side. Found in Cameroon, the western part of the Democratic Republic of the Congo, and northern Gabon. *Impatiens mackeyana* subsp. *claeri* Grey-Wilson: leaves broadly ovate to ovate-lanceolate, with indentation near the base on either side, 6–18 cm long by 3–9 cm wide, with a zone of pale variegation down the center. Found in southeastern Cameroon and central and eastern Gabon.

Impatiens meruensis Gilg

Perennial herb, decumbent to erect, growing to 50 cm high, simple to moderately branched, pubescent when young, gradually losing it with age. Leaves arranged spirally, ovate to ovate-lanceolate or elliptical, margins finely crenate to dentate, lower teeth often filiform, petioles 4–6 cm long. Flowers solitary or in pairs, 2.5–3 cm across, pale pink to mauve, upper pair of lateral petals with a purple mark at the base, lower sepal abruptly constricted into a filiform spur. Seed capsule fusiform, 1.5 cm long. *Impatiens meruensis* is found in northern Tanzania and on Mt. Kilimanjaro and Mt. Meru.

Impatiens mildbraedii Gilg

Procumbent to straggling, annual or perennial species, stems thin, rooting at the lower nodes, growing to 50 cm long, sparsely branched, finely pubescent. Leaves arranged alternately, petioled, 6 cm long by 2.5 cm wide, elliptical to ovate-lanceolate, margins crenate-dentate. Flowers pale pink, 2.5 cm across, in small racemes of two to four; lateral sepals small, linear-lanceolate, lower sepal 4–6.5 mm long, abruptly constricting into a thin, curved, spur; dorsal petal small, slightly hooded, with a narrow dorsal crest, pointed at top; lateral united petals 10–15 mm long, upper pair narrowly oblong, lower pair suborbicular to elliptical. Seed capsule fusiform, 1 cm long. *Impatiens mildbraedii* is found in the Democratic Republic of the Congo, Rwanda, Burundi, and Uganda.

Impatiens nana Engler & Warburg ex Engler

Erect to lax annual species, growing to 30–80 cm tall, stems sometimes pink-ish red, often rooting at the lower nodes, slightly pubescent. Leaves arranged alternately, sessile to subsessile, ovate to elliptical-lanceolate, margins crenate or serrate. Flowers pink to light purple, with a dark magenta mark at the base of each lateral petal, solitary or in groups of two or three, in leaf axils; lateral sepals linear, pointed, 3–5 mm long, lower sepal 1 cm long, boat-shaped, abruptly constricted into a curved, thin spur; dorsal petal almost orbicular, 1 cm in diameter, with narrow dorsal crest, pointed at front; lateral united petals 15–21 mm long, upper pair ovate to suborbicular, lower pair transversely oblong, 8 mm by 9 mm long. Seed capsule fusiform, 1.5–2.5 cm long. *Impatiens nana* is only found in Tanzania, both in the north and west of the country.

Impatiens niamniamensis Gilg

Erect perennial species with thick, succulent stems, rather densely leaved, sometimes getting woody and losing lower leaves when conditions are not favorable. Leaves arranged spirally, petiolate, petioles 1–7 cm long, often with fimbriae near the base, leaf 6–20 cm long by 4–8 cm wide, broadly

Impatiens niamniamensis

ovate-oblong or elliptical, leaf margins crenate, crenations overlapping. Flowers in fascicles of two to six, sometimes solitary, often flowering directly from bare stem, epedunculate, deeply pouched, the spur quite variable in shape and color from red and yellow to red, magenta, and pink; lateral sepals tiny, 2 mm long, reflexed, lower sepal 2–3 cm long, deeply saccate, constricted into a sharply incurving, often bilobed spur; dorsal petal small, 1 cm by 0.5 cm, hooded; lateral united petals 1–1.5 cm long, upper pair larger than the lower. Seed capsule 1.5 cm long, fusiform. *Impatiens niamniamensis* is a widely distributed species, ranging from Tanzania in the east, across through central Africa to Cameroon in the west and is even found on the offshore island of Fernando Po in the Atlantic. This species can be found growing in moist, deeply shaded areas, near rivers and streams, occasionally growing epiphytically. The "Congo cockatoo," as it is often called, is a well-known and attractive plant that has been in cultivation for a considerable time as a greenhouse pot plant. It has been offered by many nurseries worldwide for some time.

Impatiens nyungwensis E. Fischer

A procumbent, much-branched, perennial species, pubescent, growing to about 1 m in length, stems prostrate to ascending, 30–50 cm long. Leaves arranged spirally, broadly to narrowly cordate, 4.5–6 cm long by 4 cm wide, pilose above and below, margins crenate to dentate with broad teeth and short fimbriae, petiole 15–65 mm long. Flowers two to three in racemes, deep orange red with greenish dorsal petal, lower sepal greenish at the mouth, pedicel 18–20 mm long; lateral sepals 6–7 mm by 4–5 mm, ovate, pilose, lower sepal 1.5 cm wide by 3.5 cm overall length, gradually tapering into spiraled spur; dorsal petal cucullate with narrow pilose crest, terminating in short point, 12 mm by 6 mm; lateral united petals 2.2 cm long, upper petal 4 mm by 4 mm, acuminate, lower petal 15 mm by 10 mm. Seed capsule 1 cm long. Seed capsule spindle-shaped. *Impatiens nyungwensis* is only found in the Nyungwe Forest in Rwanda.

Impatiens nyungwensis

Impatiens paucidentata

Impatiens paucidentata De Wildeman

Epiphytic perennial species, growing to 40–50 cm high, lax in habit. Leaves arranged spirally, thick and fleshy, 6–10 cm long by 2–3 cm wide, broadly to narrowly elliptical to elliptical-lanceolate in texture, margins with a few widely spaced teeth and one or two glands near the base, petiolate, petioles 5–12 mm long. Flowers solitary, dark red to orange red, epedunculate; lateral sepals 2.5 mm long, linear, lower sepal 1 cm wide, bucciniform, gradually narrowing into an incurving spur, 3–4 cm long; dorsal petal 0.5–1 cm, cucullate, with broad crest ending in a short point; lateral united petals 1 cm long, the two petals equal in length. Seed capsule 1 cm long, bursiform. *Impatiens paucidentata* is only found in the eastern part of the Democratic Republic of the Congo and Uganda.

Impatiens polyantha Gilg

Upright, weakly stemmed, branched, perennial plant, growing to 40–50 cm tall. Leaves arranged spirally, sessile to shortly petioled, 2–4 cm long by 1.5 cm wide, narrowly oblong, elliptical to lanceolate, leaf edges crenulate to dentate. Flowers in fascicles of two to four but sometimes single, white or pale pink, 3–4 cm across, lowers sepal 1–2 cm long, abruptly constricted into a short spur. Seed capsule fusiform. *Impatiens polyantha* is found in southern Tanzania and northern Malawi.

Impatiens pseudoviola Gilg

A shorter, decumbent or slightly trailing species that forms a neat little mound of flowers. Leaves arranged spirally, 2.5 cm by 3.5 cm, with crenate to serrate margins. Flowers 2 cm across, lilac, with purple markings and two small, yellow spots near the center. The plant produces flowers in great abundance and can be constantly flowering. Seed capsule fusiform or spindle-shaped. *Impatiens pseudoviola* has a wide-ranging distribution in both Kenya and Tanzania. It readily hybridizes with *I. kilimanjari*, producing many colorful cultivars. There is also an albino variety, *I. pseudoviola* 'Alba'. This species is a very good plant for the front of the border, making a small mound of flowers. Many nurseries are now offering this species and some of the many hybrids.

Impatiens psychadelphoides Launert

Perennial plant with erect to decumbent stems, growing to over 1 m high, weakly branched. Leaves arranged spirally, 3–10 cm long by 3–5 cm wide, sparsely pubescent to glabrous, ovate to elliptical-lanceolate, leaf margins finely serrate-denticulate, petiole often densely pubescent. Flowers pink, solitary, rarely in fascicles of two or three, pedicels 4–5 cm long; lateral sepals 6 mm long, ovate lanceolate, lower sepal 1–1.5 mm by 0.6–0.7 mm, obliquely navicular, abruptly constricted into a 2.5- to 3.5-cm long, filiform, incurving spur, pubescent; dorsal petal 1.5 cm by 2 cm, broadly ovate, deeply emarginated at the top, with narrow dorsal crest; lateral united petals 2–3 cm long, upper petal 6–10 mm by 5–6 mm, ovate, apiculate, lower petal 1.5–2 cm by 0.9–1.4 cm, broadly ovate, oblong, emarginated along the inner edge. Seed capsule 2 cm long, fusiform. *Impatiens psychadelphoides* is only found growing in Mozambique and Zimbabwe.

Impatiens purpureo-violacea Gilg

Semi-prostrate perennial plant growing to 30–50 cm tall, rooting at the lower nodes, often densely pubescent when young and losing this pubescence as the plant grows. Leaves arranged spirally, dark green above, paler below, 3–5 cm long by 2–3 cm wide, ovate to elliptical with crenate leaf margins. Flowers in racemes of one to three, pink with a magenta spot at the base of each pair of lateral petals, 3.5–4 cm across, lower sepal abruptly constricted into a spiraled 2.5-cm spur. Seed capsule narrowly fusiform, 2 cm long. *Impatiens purpureo-violacea* is found in the Democratic Republic of the Congo, Rwanda, and Burundi.

Impatiens rosulata Grey-Wilson

A perennial species with a rather fleshy root system, which supports a crown producing usually one, but sometimes two shoots that develop into an extremely short stem 3–8 cm high, most of which is hidden below the ground, forming an unbranched rosette of leaves, glabrous, arranged spirally, very close together, sessile, lowermost leaves smaller than the upper ones, 5–18 cm long by 3–6 cm wide, oblong to oblong-elliptical or oblanceolate, shallowly serrate or crenate. Flowers solitary or in fascicles of two or three, epedunculate, white to pale pink with two yellow spots in the throat, pedicels 3–10 cm long, slender lateral sepals, 5–8 mm long by 4–6 mm wide, broadly ovate or cordate, lower sepal 12–16 mm long by 5–7 mm deep, navicular, abruptly constricted into a very short spur, 1–2 mm long; dorsal petal 15–20 mm by 10–19 mm, cucullate, with narrow dorsal crest; lateral united petals 23–38 mm long, the upper one-third the size of the lower. Seed capsule 2 cm long. *Impatiens rosulata* is only known from the Kitulo Plateau in southern Tanzania and is found growing in open grassland. It is the only truly rosulate impatiens and thus has considerable potential as a pot or patio plant.

Impatiens rothii Hooker f.

Tuberous rooted perennial species, growing to over 1 m in height, succulent, moderately branched. Leaves arranged spirally, 5–15 cm long by 2.5 cm wide, narrowly ovate to elliptical-lanceolate, margins serrate to serrulate. Flowers pouched, 4 cm across in racemes of two to six blooms, ranging from pink, orange pink, to scarlet; two pairs of lateral sepals, lower sepal 1.5–2 cm long,

Impatiens rothii

tapering to a 3- to 4.5-cm incurving spur. Seed capsule 3–4 cm long, spindle-shaped. *Impatiens rothii* is only found growing in central Ethiopia. This species may be a contender for a herbaceous border.

Impatiens sodenii Engler & Warburg

Robust, erect, almost shrubby perennial species, growing to 3 m in height, stems thick and succulent, moderately branched, glabrous, often becoming slightly woody near the base. Leaves in dense whorls of six to 10, getting rather con-

Impatiens sodenii subsp. oliveri

Impatiens sodenii subsp. sodenii

gested near the top of the stem, 15–18 cm long by 2–5 cm wide, oblanceo-late, rarely oblong, leaf margins shallowly serrate or serrulate with a few fimbriae near the base. Inflorescence one- or two-flowered, lilac or white with magenta markings in the center, although pure white variants are known, peduncle 2.5–6 cm long, pedicel 2–4.5 cm long; lateral sepals 6–8 mm long, ovate to elliptical-lanceolate, lower sepal 14–18 mm long, narrowly navicular, abruptly constricted into a 6- to 10-cm long filiform spur; dorsal petal 18–23 mm by 25–30 mm, broadly ovate to suborbicular, emarginate, with narrow dorsal crest; lateral united petals 30–37 mm long, upper petal 21–28 mm long by 17–27 mm wide, oblong or suborbicular, emarginate, lower petal 20–33 mm by 14–21 mm, oblong, slightly emarginated. Seed capsule 2.5 cm long, fusiform. *Impatiens sodenii* is found in Kenya and northern and eastern Tanzania, growing in exposed rocky habitats.

Impatiens stuhlmannii Warburg

Very similar species to *I. apiculata* in many respects. A procumbent to strag-gling perennial plant growing to 1–2 m long, rooting at the nodes. Leaves arranged spirally, petioles 1–2 cm long, ovate to elliptical, sometimes slightly pubescent, 4–14 cm long by 2.5–7.5 cm wide, edges crenate, with fimbriae near the base. Flowers are 4–5 cm across and are displayed in racemes of

Impatiens stuhlmannii subsp. *rubra* Christopher Grey-Wilson

two to six magenta or pink blooms, although red and orange variations are known. *Impatiens stuhlmannii* is a widespread species found in the Democratic Republic of the Congo, Rwanda, Burundi, Uganda, and Kenya. This species is a good plant for the garden but will need some support.

Impatiens sylvicola Burtt Davy & Greenway

Low, scrambling or erect perennial herb, stems moderately branched, rooting at the lower nodes, usually sparsely pubescent. Leaves arranged alternately, petioles 1–3.5 cm long, broadly ovate to ovate-lanceolate, margins crenate. Flowers pink, light purple, or deep mauve, with reddish blotch at base of lateral petals; lateral sepals 4–6.5 mm long, lanceolate-triangular, lower sepal 8–11 mm long, shallowly boat-shaped, abruptly constricted into a thin curved spur, 11–17 mm long; dorsal petal 8–10 mm by 9–13 mm, suborbicular, with narrow dorsal crest; lateral united petals 8–14 mm long, upper pair broadly ovate, 1 cm long, lower pair suborbicular, with a slightly extended appendage at the bottom. Seed capsule fusiform, 1.5 cm long, pubescent. *Impatiens sylvicola* is a fairly widespread species, growing in southern Malawi, Mozambique, and South Africa. Seed of this species has been available for some years.

Impatiens
teitensis
subsp. *teitensis*

Impatiens teitensis Grey-Wilson

Upright perennial species with few branches, growing to 1.5 m high. Leaves shiny dark green, in whorls or verticils of two to four, sometimes alternate, 7–12 cm long by 4–6 cm wide, elliptical to oblanceolate, edges shallowly crenate to dentate, petioles 1.5–3 cm long, slender with a few stipitate glands near the top. Flowers in a raceme of four to eight, white with dark purple markings at the base of each pair of lateral petals, lateral petals unequal, the top being half the size of the lower pair, lower sepal navicular, constricted into a filiform spur, 4.5–5.5 cm long. *Impatiens teitensis* subsp. *teitensis* is only found in Kenya. *Impatiens teitensis* subsp. *oblanceolata*, which is native to Tanzania, has more lanceolate leaves, and the lateral petals are more equal in size.

Impatiens tinctoria A. Richard

A fairly tall, tuberous, perennial plant that grows to about 2 m or more in height. Leaves arranged spirally, petioled, ovate, about 5 cm by 10 cm, with serrated margins. Flowers in raceme of three to seven blooms, each 5 cm or more across, slightly fragrant, white with pinkish magenta markings in the center; long filiform spur is the longest of any African species at over 10 cm.

Impatiens tinctoria

Seed capsule clavate or club-shaped. *Impatiens tinctoria* is found in northeastern Africa, in eastern Democratic Republic of the Congo, Sudan, Ethiopia, and Uganda. In the United Kingdom, this species flowers from midsummer to late autumn, when frost causes it to die back to its *Dahlia*-like tubers. If left undisturbed, it will eventually form large clumps from which it produces a really spectacular show. At least four subspecies are known. Many nurseries have been offering *I. tinctoria* for some time, as it makes an ideal plant for the back of the border. It is reliably hardy in warmer regions, but may need some protection in cold areas.

Impatiens usambarensis Grey-Wilson

Strong-growing plant of up to about 1 m high. Similar in many respects to *I. walleriana*, the species into which it was once included, but rather more robust, with few branches. Leaves arranged spirally, ovate, with slightly serrate edges. Flowers open faced, usually carmine red. A few hybrids with *I. wal-*

leriana are known, often with orange-red flowers and much more branched. *Impatiens usambarensis* comes from the Usambara Mountains of Tanzania. This species adapts well to patio planting.

Impatiens walleriana Hooker f.

Perennial species, growing to 70 cm tall, stems simple or branched, lower ones sometimes rooting at the nodes. Leaves spirally arranged 4–12 cm long by 2.5–5 cm wide, elliptical to ovate, sometimes with a reddish tinge, glabrous, margins crenate, petioles 1–3 cm long. Flowers in axillary racemes, usually in pairs, varying in color from orange-red to pink, purple, and white; lateral sepals two, ovate-lanceolate, 3–6 mm long, lower sepal shallowly boat-shaped, abruptly constricted into a long, thin, curved spur, 28–45 mm long; dorsal petal broadly obovate, flat, with a narrow crest on reverse side, pointed at front, 11–19 mm long by 13–25 mm wide; lateral united petals 18–25 cm long, upper petals almost equal in size to the lower ones, both obovate. Seed capsule fusiform, 1.5–2 cm long. *Impatiens walleriana* is found in southeastern Kenya, Tanzania, Zanzibar, Mozambique, and Malawi.

Impatiens zombensis Baker f.

A much-branched perennial plant, often decumbent and rooting at the nodes, growing up to 50 cm high. Leaves arranged spirally, ovate, with shallowly serrate edges. Flowers single, but occasionally in pairs, light purple, 2 cm wide. Seed capsule spindle-shaped. *Impatiens zombensis* comes from Malawi and Mozambique. This one is a very pretty species and another very good patio plant, ideally suited to containers and planters, providing a profusion of purple star-shaped flowers throughout the summer months. This species grows easily from seed, which is available from specialist seed firms.

8

Impatiens of Madagascar, the Comoro Islands, and the Seychelles

Madagascar is by far the largest island in the Indian Ocean and greater in area than the whole of Great Britain. It is a place rich in botanical diversity and a major center of impatiens development. More than 200 *Impatiens* species are known to exist on Madagascar, all of which are endemic to the island. Tremendous variation is found within these species. For instance, some have the tiniest flowers known to the genus, in a few cases as little as 2–3 mm in diameter. Although these have no interest for the horticultural trade, they certainly are botanical curiosities. Quite a large portion of the species on Madagascar have flowers that are completely spurless; these form a separate group within the genus, the section *Trimorphopetalum*. These, too, have some botanical interest but little horticultural merit. There are a great many other species from Madagascar, however, that have tremendous potential for the garden, and some under cultivation have shown the capacity to hybridize freely.

Perhaps one of the most important of these is the red-flowered *Impatiens bicaudata*, which is found on Mt. Ambre in the extreme north of the island. It is a rather robust, red-stemmed plant that grows to about 1 m in height, with red and yellow cornucopia-shaped flowers standing out in contrast to its rather dark green foliage. A well-grown plant kept in a frost-free environment can eventually develop very large, thick basal stems, as much as 8–10 cm in diameter. When in flower, such a plant makes an impressive specimen. A feature that *I. bicaudata* flowers share with a few other species is large lateral sepals and bifid, short spurs.

Opposite: Impatiens bisaccata growing in its natural habitat Yong-Ming Yuan

*Impatiens
bicaudata*
Yong-Ming Yuan

One of these species is *Impatiens tuberosa*, which is unique within the genus, being the only plant that dies back to a woody caudex during the dry season. In common with other caudiform succulents, *I. tuberosa* restarts into growth with the return of the rainy season with new growth sprouting directly from various points at the top of this caudex. It grows to about 40 cm in height and has pale lilac flowers, similar in many resects to those of *I. bicaudata*, with which it can form hybrids. *Impatiens tuberosa* can be grown easily from cuttings, but strangely these plants do not die back in the same way to form the caudex; only seed-sown plants have this ability. Although still quite rare in cultivation, *I. tuberosa* can sometimes be found in the collections of succulent enthusiasts.

The best-known of these hybrids are from crosses *Impatiens tuberosa* with *I. auricoma*, a yellow-flowered species from the Comoros. These have become known erroneously as *I.* 'African Orchid' and are available from some seed merchants. The resultant plants often show a great deal of variation, with some very nice color combinations. *Impatiens auricoma* has been known since 1893, when it was discovered as a seedling growing in a consignment of tree ferns imported into France by M. Landry. The species was described in 1894 by Henri Ernest Baillon of the Linnaean Society of Paris. *Impatiens auricoma* has been found to cross with similar species, in addition to *I. bicaudata*, to form hybrids in an endless series of color combinations that are surely destined to become popular and more widely available.

Impatiens catatii is a truly spectacular species and one deserved of a place in any summer garden. This is a medium-sized plant, growing to 60–70 cm high. It bears whorls of scarlet, trumpet-shaped flowers between the axils of its dark green leaves at regular intervals along the length of the stems. The flowers are about 3–4 cm long and are very attractive. A similar species is *I. eriosperma*, which also has whorled foliage, but with not quite so many flowers on the stem. Because it is a bushier plant, however, it produces just as fine a show as *I. catatii*. *Impatiens eriosperma* also has trumpet-shaped flowers, but differs by having a shorter, more incurving spur. Both these species flower continuously; if brought indoors during the winter months, they will provide color all year round.

Another fine, recently described species is *Impatiens emilia*. It is a tall plant reaching about 1 m in height, with, bright orange, flat-faced flowers, standing out from whorls of dark green leaves. The species resembles a tall New Guinea hybrid, but it is not yet available in the trade.

Impatiens lyallii is an extremely varied species with purple to pale lilac, flat flowers, some with paler markings near the center, and with long white spurs. Because its habit varies from erect to somewhat trailing, this species could be useful as a patio plant.

Among the spurless species, there are many unusual looking plants reminiscent of species orchids. Not blessed with great beauty, their colors are sometimes a rather drab light green or various shades of brown, but the interest stems from their intricate markings, often with pronounced dark veining or spotting. The spurless *Impatiens begonioides* is very unusual in having peltate leaves, in which the petiole (leaf stalk) joins the leaf at a point underneath instead of at the end, as in other species. Only one other species in the genus shares this characteristic, *I. peltata*, which grows on the Malay Peninsula. The flowers of *I. begonioides* are pale green, heavily peppered with tiny, raised black spots, giving it a slightly sinister appearance. The fleshy dark green leaves have lighter green markings. Most of the spurless species are small, and the habit is ground-hugging and creeping or trailing.

The Comoros are a group of volcanic islands forming an archipelago to the northwest of Madagascar. Most are little more than islets, although the four main islands are quite large. The nearest of these is less than 320 km away from the Madagascan coast. Considering the close proximity of the Comoros, relatively few *Impatiens* species have been found there. The best known of these is *I. auricoma*, a species that has been in general cultivation for almost a century. In recent years, *I. auricoma* has been extremely important to plant breeders due to it having bright yellow flowers, and it has been used in crosses to produce many new interspecific hybrids.

The Seychelles is another group of islands still further north of Madagascar in the Indian Ocean, of which Mahé is the largest. Although Mahé has now become a holiday playground, it does have one endemic species, *Impatiens gordonii*, named in honor of Gen. Charles Gordon, who once held camp there during his campaigns. Due to the growth of agriculture and tourism, the species was on the verge of extinction in the 1980s, and only a few plants remained. Steps were taken by the government agencies, and Kew was asked to help. Today, with the help of the Eden Project, things are looking much brighter, and hundreds of new plants have been reintroduced to the island.

The Species

Impatiens andringitrensis H. Perrier

Slender, erect, or trailing perennial plant, branching, all parts covered in short hairs. Leaves broadly ovate, arranged alternately, edges crenate. Flowers very small, 4.5 mm across, green with purple marking on lateral petals. This species is found on Madagascar.

Impatiens auricoma Baillon

Impatiens auricoma

Succulent, erect, strongly branched perennial plant, smooth or glabrous in all parts, growing to 40–50 cm high, stems and branches thick, often reddish. Leaves 12–15 cm long by 3–5 cm wide, arranged alternately, leaf edges crenate, petioles 3–4 cm long, bright green. Flowers cupped or pouched, golden yellow with some red streaking in the throat, 3 cm; lateral sepals two, orbicular, 75 mm long, concave, lower sepal short, incurving with forked short spur; dorsal petal orbicular, with dorsal keel coming to a point at the front; lateral united petals oblong, lower smaller. Seed capsule 2 cm, spindle-shaped. *Impatiens auricoma* is endemic to the Comoros and has been in cultivation for a great many years. It is a particularly beautiful species and has been used in producing interspecific hybrids.

Impatiens auricoma var. 2

A varietal form of *I. auricoma*, with white flowers and pink dorsal petal and sepals. The lateral sepals slightly reflexed. This variety is found only on the Comoro Islands.

Impatiens baroni Baker

A quite variable annual plant, upright, branching, growing to 30–60 cm in height, stems reddish. Leaves arranged alternately, widely spaced, oval, 3 cm long by 2 cm wide, shallowly serrated. Flowers open faced, dark rose to mauve, single or in pairs; lateral sepals small, lower sepal 2 cm, abruptly constricted into a short 2-cm spur; dorsal petal small, deeply hooded; lateral united petals 2 cm long, upper very small, cupped, lower much larger, orbicular, 1 cm across. Seed capsule 1 cm, spindle-shaped. *Impatiens baronii* is a very common annual plant found in central areas of Madagascar.

Impatiens begonioides E. Fischer & Rahelivololona

Decumbent to erect herb, growing to 15–30 cm high, spreading by runners through the leaf litter on the forest floor. Leaves 3 cm long by 2 cm wide, arranged alternately, peltate, dark green with lighter green markings, pale green on undersides, petioles 2–3 cm long, edges shallowly dentate. Flowers pale yellowish green, with minute, black raised spots crowded on lateral

Impatiens begonioides

petals; lateral sepals two, tiny, lower sepal 1–0.5 cm, with some veining, no spur; dorsal petal orbicular, 1 cm wide, heavily hooded, strongly veined dark purple; lateral united petals 15–20 mm long, upper small, dark veining, lower 1 cm, orbicular, with heavy dark spotting. Seed capsule unknown. *Impatiens begonioides* is mainly found in the Ranomafana National Park area.

Impatiens bicaudata H. Perrier

An erect perennial herb, branched with thick, succulent, red stems, growing to a height of 1–1.5 m. Leaves arranged alternately, dark green, shiny, often with red midrib, 7–16 cm by 3–5 cm, serrated edges. Flowers large, pouched, bright red, lower sepal and spur shading to white, bright yellow area in the throat; lateral sepals two, large, 1 cm by 1 cm, oval, lower sepal 10–15 mm long, tapering into a strongly incurving, forked spur; dorsal petal hooded, with large dorsal keel, coming to a point at the front; lateral united petals small. Anthers covered with purple pollen. Seed capsule 2 cm long, spindle-shaped. *Impatiens bicaudata* is only found in the northern mountainous part of Madagascar. It is a very impressive plant that does well in the garden, but must be described as half-hardy. When grown in large pots with frost protection, it can eventually produce basal stems 8–10 cm in diameter.

Impatiens bisaccata Warburg

Erect, branching plant, growing to 80 cm in height, often losing leaves lower down, tending to bunch near the top, leaving somewhat bare stems. Leaves large, 10–15 cm long by 3–6 cm wide, smooth, arranged alternately, with long petioles, leaf edges serrated. Flowers semi-pouched, rose-purple, single, sometimes in pairs; lateral sepals two, orbicular, small, lower sepal wide and short, with bisaccate spur, conspicuously transverse markings in the throat; dorsal petal rounded, 1 cm; lateral united petals 1.5–2 cm long. Seed capsule spindle-shaped. *Impatiens bisaccata* is found in central and northern parts of Madagascar, especially on Mt. Ambre.

Impatiens catatii Baillon

An erect, subshrubby, weakly branched plant, growing to 70–90 cm in height. Leaves arranged in whorls of four to six, dark green above, paler green below, lanceolate, shiny, edges shallowly serrated, with serrations widely spaced. Flowers in the axils of the leaves in groups of three to seven, one to each leaf axil, bright red throughout, pouched; dorsal petal hooded, 1 cm by 1 cm, lateral petals small, lower sepal tapering to a narrowly incurving spur. Seed

*Impatiens
bicaudata*
Yong-Ming Yuan

*Impatiens
catatii*

Impatiens decaryana

capsule 3 cm long, spindle-shaped. *Impatiens catatii* is found in the eastern forests of Madagascar near rivers and streams. This is a particularly attractive plant that should make a fine addition to any summer garden.

Impatiens decaryana H. Perrier

Small low-growing, semi-erect herb, branching, growing to 20–30 cm in height, smooth in all parts. Leaves ovate-oblong, 4 cm long by 2 cm wide, pale green sometimes with a slight metallic sheen, leaf edges crenate. Flowers pale green, with intricate netting of dark colored veining on the lateral petals; dorsal petal narrowly hooded, lateral petals 2 cm wide, lower sepal short and spurless. Seed capsule unknown. *Impatiens decaryana* is found in central areas of Madagascar, usually growing on damp rocks in forests.

Impatiens eriosperma

Impatiens eriosperma H. Perrier

Erect, spindly, sometimes lightly branched, almost shrubby species, growing to about 1 m in height, sometimes epiphytic. Leaves in verticils of three to six, 6–8 cm long by 2–3 cm wide, glabrous, oblong or oblong-lanceolate, petiolate, crenate, large crenatures. Flowers red or mauve, usually solitary, epedunculate, almost flat-faced, sepals two, small ovoid, lower sepal gradually narrowing into a thin, very incurved spur; dorsal petal large, 1.5 cm wide, ovoid, slightly hooded, lateral petals 2 cm long, upper slightly larger than lower pair. Seed capsule fusiform, 2 cm long. *Impatiens eriosperma* is usually found in central Madagascar on Mt. Tsaratanana. This is a very useful and colorful plant for the garden, and some nurseries have begun to offer it in their lists.

Impatiens firmula Baker

Small, branched, slightly woody, perennial plant, spindly or flexuose. Leaves shiny, dark green, sometimes tinged with purple, 2–3 cm long by 1 cm wide. Flowers mauve to pinkish red, sometimes touched with darker color; dorsal petal 7–10 mm across, lateral petals 2 cm, lower sepal 25–50 mm long. Seed capsule 1.5 cm long, narrowed at both ends. *Impatiens firmula* is another fairly widespread species, found mainly in western Madagascar, usually in damp, wooded areas.

Impatiens gordonii Horne

Erect, rather branched perennial species growing to about 60 cm tall, stems green, sometimes flushed pink. Leaves arranged spirally, broadly ovate to elliptical, 8–10 cm long by 4–5 cm wide, edges serrated. Flowers in racemes of two to three, white with pinkish center, purple pollen and a bright pink spur, flowers held erect lateral sepals two, ovate, 5 cm long, lower sepal boat-shaped, narrowly constricted into a long, slender, filiform spur, 6–7 cm long; dorsal petal almost heart-shaped, 2 cm by 2 cm broad; lateral united petals 2.5–3 cm long, lower petals as long as the upper petals, but narrower, 2 cm long. Seed capsule fusiform, 2 cm long. *Impatiens gordonii* is only found in the Seychelles, on the islands of Mahé and Silhouette, in montane rain forest.

Impatiens inaperta (H. Perrier) H. Perrier

A very small, branched plant, growing to no more than 10 cm high. Leaves 1 cm by 0.5 cm, light green, serrated. Flowers tiny or more often cleistogamous (progressing from the bud stage directly to seed capsule). Seed capsule 0.5 cm long. Two distinct varieties are known: *I. inaperta* var. *glabra* differs by having two thin lines down the center of the leaves, and *I. inaperta* var. *longipetiolata* has larger, brown, hairy leaves and stems.

Impatiens laurentii E. Fischer & Rahelivololona

Erect, branched, succulent, perennial species, growing to 50–60 cm high. Leaves pale green, arranged alternately, 8 cm long by 3 cm wide, shallowly serrate, petioles 3 cm long. Flowers light pink, with some deep red striping in the throat, flat-faced; lateral sepals ovate, 4 mm long, lower sepal constricted into a filiform spur, 4 cm long; dorsal petal orbicular, 2 cm across; lateral united petals orbicular, 2.5 cm. Seed capsule spindle-shaped, 2 cm long. *Impatiens laurentii* is only found in northeastern Madagascar at Daraina.

Impatiens lyallii Baker

Branched, upright or semi-erect, lax herb, growing to 60 cm or more in height, all parts slightly hairy. Leaves arranged alternately, widely separated, 9 cm long by 3 cm wide, oblong. Flowers flat-faced, mauve to light rose, single or in groups of two or three; dorsal petal 7–8 mm across; lateral united petals 17–25 mm across, lower sepal tapering into a long, thin white spur, 25–40

*Impatiens
laurentii*

mm long. Seed capsule 25 mm long. *Impatiens lyallii* is a common species, widespread in central and eastern areas of Madagascar, found growing in woods and mossy forests. It is a quite variable species, and many varieties are recognized.

Impatiens malcomberi E. Fischer & Rahelivololona

Epiphytic, branched herb with fleshy reddish stems, growing to 25–30 cm high. Leaves arranged alternately, oval, 6–10 cm long by 3–3.5 cm wide, leaf edges serrated, petioles 15–20 mm long. Flowers bright yellow, with dark purplish veins; lateral sepals two, thin, pointed, lower sepal short and pointed; dorsal petal hooded, 1 cm by 0.25 cm; lateral united petals 1 cm long, upper shorter than the lower. Seed capsule unknown. *Impatiens malcomberi* is found in the north of Madagascar, in Mt. Ambre National Park.

Impatiens mandrakae E. Fischer & Rahelivololona

Procumbent or trailing plant, growing to 30 cm long, glabrous in all parts, rooting at the nodes where they touch the ground. Leaves dark green, sometimes pinkish, petioles 1–2.5 cm in length, leaf size 4 cm long by 2 cm wide, edges slightly serrated. Flowers very small, translucent green; lateral sepals tiny, lower sepal ovate, 5 mm by 3 mm; dorsal petal 4 mm by 3 mm, lateral petals 9–11 mm, linear. Seed capsule unknown. This species grows on Mt. Fody in the Mangoro Basin of Madagascar.

Impatiens masoalensis H. Perrier

Small plant, growing to 15 cm high, slightly hairy on young foliage, simple habit, but slightly branched lower down on stem, rooting at nodes. Leaves dark green on top, reddish below, 4–5 cm long, crenate. Flowers small, 2 cm; lateral sepals reddish outside, yellowish inside, lower sepal small with short spur; dorsal petal deeply hooded, lateral petals 1.5 cm, pale to deep mauve, clear yellow at base, deep red in throat. Seed capsule fusiform, 1.5 cm long. *Impatiens masoalensis* is only found in eastern Madagascar, in forests on the massif of Masoala.

Impatiens mindiae E. Fischer & Rahelivololona

Erect herb, growing to 45 cm in height. Leaves 7 cm long by 2.5 cm wide, shallowly crenate. Flowers 3.5 cm across, white and deep rose; lateral sepals 7 mm by 2 mm, lower sepal boat-shaped, 1.5 cm by 0.5 cm, abruptly constricted into a strongly incurving narrow spur, 1 cm long; dorsal petal white, with some red spotting, hooded, 1.5 cm by 1 cm, with a 5-mm spur at apex, lateral petals with two yellow spots at the center, deep rose, 2.5 cm long, upper 1 cm by 0.5 cm, lower petal bilobed, 1.7 cm by 1.5 cm. Seed capsule unknown. *Impatiens mindiae* is found on the Masoala Peninsular Reserve of Madagascar, in montane bamboo evergreen forests.

Impatiens navicula E. Fischer & Rahelivololona

Small erect herb, densely hairy in all parts, growing to 6 cm tall. Leaves 2 cm long by 1.5 cm wide, ovate to orbicular, underside of leaf pale green, upper side darker green, edges serrated with four or five teeth each side. Flowers hidden by leaves, dark brown, nodding; lateral sepals tiny, greenish brown and hairy, lower sepal 8 mm by 9 mm, dark green with purple veins; dorsal petal 8 mm by 7 mm, dark green with reddish brown veining, hairy dorsal crest, lateral petals 8–9 mm long, dark chocolate brown. Seed capsule *Impatiens navicula* is found growing in moss in mountainous rain forest at Marojejy massif on Madagascar.

Impatiens rutenbergii O. Hoffmann

Erect, rhizomatous, perennial species, with simple unbranched stems, growing to 40–60 cm tall. Leaves narrow, 6–8 cm long by 1 cm wide, arranged alternately, very close together on the stem, short petioles, edges serrated, smooth. Flowers flat, pale pink to dark mauve, single; dorsal petal 15 mm wide, lateral petals large, 3 cm across. Seed capsule spindular, seeds reddish, smooth. *Impatiens rutenbergii* is found in the central parts of Madagascar.

Impatiens substipulata H. Perrier

Tuberous (tubers 3–4 cm in diameter), upright, little branched species, with thin stems, swollen at nodes, and growing to 30–40 cm high. Leaves arranged alternately, dark velvety green above, lighter green below, 6 cm long by 3 cm wide, ovate, edges serrate. Flowers flat-faced, light purple with white blotch at the center, 3–4 cm across, small lateral sepals, lower sepal tapering to a thin straight spur, 2.5 cm long; dorsal petal orbicular, 1.5–2 cm in diameter; lateral united petals orbicular, upper 1 cm, lower 1 cm. Seed capsule spindle-shaped. *Impatiens substipulata* is usually found in hilly, wooded areas in central Madagascar.

Impatiens tuberosa H. Perrier

Tuberous species, tuber (or caudex) 3–7 cm diameter, with annual stems rising from points at the top, fleshy, with little branching, growing to 40–50 cm high. Leaves 5 cm long by 3 cm wide, edges crenate. Flowers pouched, in pairs, pale rose and white, 2–2.5 cm; lateral sepals two, ovate to lanceolate, 7.5 mm long, lower sepal short, strongly incurving, with short forked spur; dorsal petal hooded, lateral petals two, small, 2 cm long. *Impatiens tuberosa* is found on the northern areas of Madagascar in Antsiranana Province, usually on dry, shady, chalky rocks. Plants die back to the tuberous caudex annually at the end of the growing season, increasing in size with age.

Impatiens tuberosa

Impatiens vilersi Costantin & Poisson

Tall, upright, shrubby perennial species, growing to 2 m high, slightly hairy stems and undersides of leaves. Leaves arranged oppositely or in whorls of three to six, smooth above, 5–10 cm long by 2–5 cm wide, ovate to oblong. Flowers large, flat-faced, light rose, 3–4 cm, single or in groups of two or three; lateral sepals two, ovate to lanceolate, lower sepal 1–1.5 cm, abruptly constricted into a long thin spur, 3–5.5 cm long; dorsal petal 7 mm by 3 mm, lateral petals 2 cm. Seed capsule unknown. *Impatiens vilersi* is found in the central and eastern parts of Madagascar.

Impatiens wibkeae E. Fischer & Rahelivololona

Epiphytic herb with succulent stem, growing to 60 cm tall. Leaves dark green, ovate, 10 cm long by 4 cm wide, petiole 2.5–3 cm long. Flowers yellow and orange-red; lateral sepals broadly ovate, 3 cm long by 1 cm wide, orange-red, lower sepal boat-shaped, with short bilobed spur; dorsal petal hooded, 2 cm by 1.5 cm, with red-tinged dorsal crest; lateral united petals 2.4 cm long. Seed capsule 2 cm long. *Impatiens wibkeae* is found growing in the rain forests of the Comoros. In many respects, this species resembles *I. auricoma*.

9

Impatiens of the Himalayas

The vast Himalayan mountain range stretches from Tibet in the north to India in the south and from Nepal in the west to China in the east. The foothills of the Himalayas are one of the most important areas of proliferation of the genus *Impatiens*. Isolated geographically from other major impatiens populations, the Himalayan species have evolved in different ways. Due to the extreme seasonal temperature differences, most are annual species, although there are some perennial Himalayan species, increasingly so as we move toward the more easterly regions.

Many of these plants were brought to us by the intrepid plant hunters of the past and introduced into our gardens in bygone days. Sadly, most of them have not become popular in the horticultural trade, with the notable exception of *Impatiens glandulifera*, the "policeman's helmet." This species is a notoriously invasive and prolific wildflower, outgrowing its welcome by covering large areas of waterside land throughout the British countryside and proving to be very difficult to control. Many less-invasive Himalayan species are now being reintroduced into cultivation, however, mainly through the rare plant trade, and new ones are being discovered continuously.

Only a fraction of the *Impatiens* species that inhabit these areas have been described, probably about 300 so far, but doubtless a great many more are waiting to be discovered. Indeed, it looks as though we may have only just scratched the surface. Most of the known species were described more than a century ago, many by the great man himself, J. D. Hooker, who described about 200 Himalayan species. With easier access and travel, dozens of plant

Opposite: Typical Himalayan impatiens habitat
Yong-Ming Yuan

hunters visit the Himalayas yearly, returning with many new plants, including some that had been lost to cultivation for a long time.

Many of the Himalayan species are very colorful, and their long flowering season makes them fine additions to the garden. Although *Impatiens glandulifera* is now regarded as a invasive wildflower, it can be worthwhile growing as it makes a tall, free-flowering plant, over 2 m high, ideal for the back of the border. An even better plant is *I. candida*, almost identical in appearance, but with spectacular white flowers with some yellow spotting in the throat. These two are abundant self-seeders, but they can easily be controlled. Both are now being offered in many seed catalogues.

An increasing number of companies are offering other annual species, such as *Impatiens balfourii*, *I. scabrida*, *I. edgeworthii*, and *I. falcifer*. *Impatiens balfourii* is well worth growing, as it reaches 60–70 cm in height and is covered with showy pink and white flowers throughout the summer. *Impatiens scabrida* and *I. edgeworthii*, no less floriferous, are much taller, at over 1 m high. They produce yellow and cream flowers, with some red or brown spotting at the center. *Impatiens falcifer* can be a little straggling, but nonetheless it has lovely, bright yellow, open flowers, often with some red spotting on the dorsal and upper lateral petals. All of these plants have a long flowering season that ends with the first frosts.

Many more Himalayan species have yet to be introduced to the trade. The attractive *Impatiens delavayi* produces large purple and yellow blooms, and *I. soulieana* bears dozens of lemon yellow flowers. The yellow-flowered species *I. racemosa*, which comes from Nepal, has dark green, reddish tinged foliage, showing off its flowers really well.

A few nurseries are now offering some perennial Himalayan species. *Impatiens arguta* is an exceptionally good plant, being hardy in most parts of Britain and the United States. It grows to 60 cm tall and covers itself with large lilac blue to mauve flowers throughout the summer. *Impatiens arguta* is a widespread species found in northern India, Nepal, southern China, and Tibet, and it exhibits some regional differences in flower color and height. There is also a pure white-flowered form, *I. arguta* var. *alba*, which is just as floriferous. *Impatiens stenantha* is another good perennial species that is almost as widespread as *I. arguta* and inhabits many of the same locations throughout the Himalayan range. *Impatiens stenantha* grows to 30 cm in height and produces yellow flowers in small umbels of two or three, usually with some dark red spotting on the petals and its rather odd upturned spur, which is highlighted against the plant's rather dark green foliage. The plant is well worth growing, as it is constantly flowering and has proven to be reliably hardy in most parts of Britain and the United States.

Recently a new species from China, collected by Don Jacobs on Mt. Emei (formerly Mt. Omei) in Sichuan Province, was introduced to the trade. The species was soon identified as *Impatiens omeiana*, which had been described more than a century earlier by J. D. Hooker. *Impatiens omeiana* is a rather lovely plant worthy of a place in any garden. It has dark green foliage with a cream, herringbone stripe running down the center of its leaves. Growing to 30–40 cm tall, the plant produces large, pouched, apricot colored flowers, 5–6 cm in length and grouped in panicles of six to eight blooms. Although it tends to flower only from late summer to early autumn, *I. omeiana* is worth growing for its foliage display alone. Recently, nurseries have been offering a close relative of this plant; it is as yet undescribed but is being sold as a variety of *I. omeiana*. Although the flowers are identical in shape and size, the color is decidedly paler. The growth habit is the same, as is the flowering period, but the foliage is a lighter shade of green, with a band of silver sheen running down the center of the leaf. Both plants are reliably hardy in most parts of Britain and the United States and are strong growers, so they should be divided periodically.

Several other Chinese species also have been collected recently but have yet to appear in nurserymen's lists. *Impatiens oxyanthera* is a fairly large-flowered, perennial species found growing on Mt. Emei. Like *I. omeiana*, this species grows from small tuberous roots and appears to be fully hardy. The light greenish pink flowers with slightly reddish markings inside the throat stand out from the rather light green leaves. Unlike *I. omeiana*, however, *I. oxyanthera* flowers throughout the summer months.

Impatiens namchabarwensis is a recently described species from Tibet found growing in the deepest canyon on earth, the Great Namchabarwa Canyon. This canyon, nearly three times the depth of the Grand Canyon of the western United States, was unknown to Western scientists until 1996, when it was discovered by a team of Chinese and American geographers. *Impatiens namchabarwensis* is destined to become one of the most popular of all garden impatiens, producing a nonstop profusion of beautiful ultramarine blue flowers. It is the only known truly blue-flowered species. Although this species is half-hardy, it makes an ideal garden plant as it self-seeds quite well. *Impatiens namchabarwensis* is becoming available from some nurseries.

The Species

Impatiens species,
Yunnan Province

Impatiens species Yunnan Province

Small, creeping or trailing perennial plant, setose in all parts. Leaves alternate, ovate, 5–7.5 cm long by 3–4 cm wide, sessile, margins crenate. Flowers solitary, bright yellow, with central red markings on upper and lower lateral petals, pedicel very hairy; lateral sepals two, small, ovate, pale green, lower sepal funnel-shaped, constricting into narrow incurving spur; dorsal petal orbicular, 1 cm; lateral united petals upper orbicular, lower wider and longer with wide dorsal auricle. Seed capsule unknown. This species is only found in Yunnan Province.

Impatiens amphorata Edgeworth

Tall, erect, much-branched, succulent, annual species, growing to almost 2 m high, with thick stems. Leaves 7.5–15 cm long, arranged alternately, petioles with stipular glands, elliptical to ovate, edges finely serrate, bright green, often with pink edges and midrib. Flowers in racemes of many flowers in upper axils, 3–4 cm long, pale purple, suffused and spotted in rose red; lateral sepals greenish, orbicular, pointed, lower sepal saccate, 2.5 cm long, abruptly constricted into a thin, incurving spur, ending in a swollen lobule; dorsal petal orbicular, bilobed, notched at the top, with dorsal crest, lateral petals 2 cm long, upper petal rounded, lower petal larger and pendulous. Seed capsule linear, 4 cm long, seed blackish. *Impatiens amphorata* is a common plant in the western Himalayas, from Kashmir to Nepal, usually at elevations around 2000 m.

Impatiens amplexicaulis Edgeworth

Robust, erect annual species, growing to 20–40 cm tall, stem often square to nearly round in cross section, with glands at the nodes, succulent, glabrous, simple or with few branches. Leaves opposite below, alternate above, sessile, oblong to oblong-lanceolate, 5–15 cm long by 2.5–5 cm wide, glabrous, margins crenate-serrate, amplexicaudal, with globose basal glands' teeth pointed. Flowers pink or pinkish purple in six- to 12-flowered umbels in leaf axils; lateral sepals two, obliquely orbicular, lower sepal obliquely saccate, abruptly narrowing into a short spur; dorsal petal suborbicular, with dorsal crest, apex pointed; lateral united petals 3 cm, upper petals suborbicular, pointed, lower petals ovate, spotted. Seed capsule linear, 2.5–3 cm long. *Impatiens amplexicaulis* can be found growing in Tibet, Nepal, and northern India.

Impatiens apsotis Hooker f.

Annual herb, growing to 10–30 cm high, stems slender, simple or sparsely branched. Leaves alternate, ovate, 3.5 cm long by 1.5–2.5 cm wide, membranous, margins coarsely crenate, petioles 1.5 cm long. Flowers white with red markings in the center, 1 cm in diameter, solitary or in pairs, in leaf axils; lateral sepals two, green, linear, lower sepal navicular, base narrowing into an incurved spur; dorsal petal orbicular, 0.5 cm, with dorsal keel, heavily hooded, lateral petals 1 cm long, upper petals small, ovate, lower petals much larger, dolabriform. Seed capsule linear, 2–3 cm long. *Impatiens apsotis* is only found in Sichuan Province and Tibet.

Impatiens aquatilis Hooker f.

Erect, annual species, sometimes purple tinged, slender but ridged, growing to 50 cm in height, rooting at nodes, simple or sparsely branched. Leaves alternate, subsessile, often with two basal glands, lanceolate to ovate-lanceolate to elliptical-ovate, 5–12 cm long by 1.5–3 cm wide, thin, leaf margins crenate to serrulate. Flowers pinkish purple with some yellow in throat, 3.5–4 cm long, in erect inflorescences of five to 10 in upper leaf axils overtopping leaves; lateral sepals two, obliquely ovate, 1 cm, lower sepal saccate, 3–3.5 cm long, gradually narrowing into an incurved spur, 2 cm long; dorsal petal orbicular, 1.2 cm in diameter; lateral united petals 2–2.5 cm long, upper petals orbicular, lower petals oblong, wider at the bottom, double the size of the top pair. Seed capsule linear, 1.5–2 cm long. *Impatiens aquatilis* is only found in Yunnan Province.

Impatiens arguta Hooker f. & Thomson

An erect, upright, branched, perennial herb, growing to about 70 cm tall. Leaves arranged alternately, 5–15 cm long by 3–5 cm wide, ovate with two stipular glands at the base of petiole, edges sharply serrate, with short teeth. Flowers 3–4 cm long, single or in pairs, light purple or mauve with white and yellow marks at the throat; sepals four, outer almost ovate, inner narrowly lanceolate, lower sepal deeply saccate, abruptly constricted into a short thin incurving spur; dorsal petal orbicular with dorsal keel, pointed at the front; lateral united petals 2.5 cm long, upper orbicular, lower petals longer and rounded. Seed capsule linear, 2.5 cm long. *Impatiens arguta* is another very widespread

*Impatiens
arguta*

*Impatiens
arguta
var. alba*

species, found growing in northern India, Nepal, Sikkim, and Yunnan. This species has been used medicinally for treating a variety of ailments.

Nurseries in Europe and the United states have been offering *Impatiens arguta* for many years. It makes a very attractive garden plant, flowering throughout the summer months, and it appears to be quite hardy in most locations. Several varietal forms are known, specific to different locations, including the white-flowered *I. arguta* var. *alba* from Yunnan Province, which is particularly attractive.

Impatiens aureliana Hooker f.

Small, erect herb, growing to 20 cm tall, simple. Leaves arranged alternately, upper surface light green, lower surface very pale green to white, ovate-lanceolate, 3.5 cm long by 1.5–2 cm wide, rigid, slightly pubescent, margins inconspicuously crenate, petioles 5–12 mm long. Flowers light purple, in upper leaf axils, solitary, 2 cm wide; lateral sepals two, narrowly pointed, 1–1.5 mm long, lower sepal navicular, abruptly narrowing into a slender spur, 1.3 cm long; dorsal petal broadly obovate, 9 mm wide by 12 mm long, bilobed, with slight dorsal crest; lateral united petals short, 1.2 cm long, upper pair broadly oblong, 9 mm by 5 mm, apex emarginated, lower petals triangular-ovate, 8 mm with suborbicular dorsal auricle. Seed capsule fusiform, 1.5 cm long, tomentose. *Impatiens aureliana* is found in broad-leaved forests and riverbanks in southwestern Yunnan Province.

Impatiens balansae Hooker f.

Perennial herb, growing to 40–60 cm in height, stem erect, robust, branched. Leaves arranged alternately, dark green, ovate, oblong or elliptical, 12–15 cm long by 5–6.5 cm wide, rigidly membranous, with one or two stipular glands, margins serrulate. Flowers yellow, large, 4–5 cm, in a terminal position or in upper leaf axils, in racemes of numerous flowers; lateral sepals four, outer two subovate, 1.5–2 cm long by 5–6 mm, apex pointed, inner pair linear oblong, 15 mm by 3–4 mm, pointed, lower sepal saccate, funnel-shaped, 3–3.5 cm long narrowing into an incurved spur, half as long as sepal; dorsal petal elliptical to obovate, 1.2 cm across, pointed at the top; lateral united petals 2.5 cm long, upper pair obovate, lower pair longer, curved, dolabriform. Seed capsule unknown. *Impatiens balansae* is found in southern Yunnan Province.

Impatiens balfourii

Impatiens balfourii Hooker f.

An upright, branched annual plant, growing to 50–70 cm high. Leaves 7.5–12 cm long, arranged alternately, shortly petioled, ovate, and minutely serrulate with somewhat recurved teeth, pale green, shiny surface, stipular glands. Flowers in racemes of six to eight, white and pink; lateral sepals two, nearly orbicular, pointed, 0.5 mm wide, lower sepal 3–5 cm long, funnel-shaped, gradually narrowing into a slightly thickened spur; dorsal petal orbicular, reflexed, white suffused with rose, with red dorsal keel, lateral petals 2.5–3 cm long, basal lobe pale yellow, lower petal much larger, hatchet-shaped, bright rose with rounded tip. Seed capsule erect, linear, 3–5 cm long, seed oblong. *Impatiens balfourii* can be found growing in the western Himalayas, Pakistan, northern India, and Nepal.

Impatiens barbata H. F. Comber

Erect, annual herb, growing to 30–45 cm high, stems simple or branched above. Leaves arranged alternately, dark green above, light green beneath, elliptical or ovate-elliptical, 5–12 cm long by 2–2.5 cm wide, membranous, sparsely pilose, margins coarsely crenate, teeth pointed, petioles 5–5.5 cm long. Flowers yellowish, large, 4 cm long, in three-flowered racemes, in upper leaf axils; lateral sepals four, outer pair obliquely ovate, 8 mm by 4 mm, inner pair linear, the same length as the outer ones, lower sepal saccate, 2 cm, narrowing to an incurving, bifid spur; dorsal petal orbicular, 2 cm in diameter, dorsally pubescent; lateral united petals 2–2.5 cm, upper petals orbicular, lower petals dolabriform, larger, pointed, with a large dorsal auricle. Seed capsule linear, 2–2.5 cm long. *Impatiens barbata* is found in southwestern Sichuan Province and northwestern Yunnan Province.

Impatiens barbata
Yong-Ming Yuan

Impatiens begoniifolia S. Akiyama & H. Ohba

An erect, annual herb, growing to 15–30 cm high, slender, with a few support-ing roots, simple. Leaves arranged alternately, dark green on upper surface, grayish green underneath, elliptical to ovate, 3–6 cm long by 1.5–3 cm wide, top surface glabrous, undersides pilose, margins shallowly crenate, petioles 5–25 mm long. Flowers pink, 3 cm, in pairs in upper leaf axils; lateral sepals two, lanceolate-ovate, 4 mm long, pointed, lower sepal pink-white, boat-shaped, base constricted into an erect spur, 1.5 cm long; dorsal petal orbicu-lar, 1 cm in diameter, with dorsal crest, emarginated at apex; lateral united petals 2.6 cm long, upper pair broadly ovate, apex rounded, lower pair ovate-dolabriform, 1.8 cm long, apex rounded. Seed capsule club-shaped. *Impatiens begoniifolia* is only found in Yunnan Province.

Impatiens bicornuta Wallich

Erect annual species, growing to about 1 m high, stems robust, succulent, glabrous, branched. Leaves alternate, 8–15 cm long by 4–5 cm wide, oblong-ovate, or broadly lanceolate, margins crenate, nearly glabrous, but with short, thick hairs on upper surface, petioled. Flowers pale purple or yellow-ish white, shaded pale purple, sometimes with reddish purple dots, in long racemes of 10–25 flowers; lateral sepals two, ovate, 4–6 mm long, pointed, lower sepal saccate, 20–25 mm long, curved downward, abruptly constricted into a spur, 3–4 mm long; dorsal petal pale purple with purple dots, hooded, 1 cm long by 1.5 cm wide; lateral united petals 32–40 mm long, upper petals ovate, 11–13 mm long, lower petals bilobed, with an appendage at inner basal part, 20–27 mm long, long tailed distally. Seed capsule linear, 2–3 cm long. *Impatiens bicornuta* is found in grasslands along rivers in northwestern India, Nepal, and Tibet.

Impatiens chinensis Linnaeus

Annual herb with erect stems above, prostrate below, rooting at the nodes, growing to 30–60 cm high, slender. Leaves oppositely arranged, sessile or with very short petioles, dark green, linear-lanceolate, 2–10 cm long by 1 cm wide, thickly textured, margins remotely serrate. Flowers variable, from pur-ple red to white, fairly large, single or in pairs, in leaf axils; lateral sepals two, linear, 1 cm long, lower sepal funnel-shaped, 1.5 cm long, with some striping, gradually tapering into a narrow, slender incurving spur; dorsal petal orbic-ular, 1–1.5 cm in diameter, with narrow dorsal crest; lateral united petals 1.5

cm, orbicular, small, lower pair much larger and wider. Seed capsule swollen at the center, 2 cm long. *Impatiens chinensis* is an extremely widespread species found growing in many parts of China, Thailand, Vietnam, and India, favoring swamps, ponds, and river edges.

Impatiens compta Hooker f.

A robust, erect, annual species, growing to about 1 m in height. Leaves arranged alternately, 3–10 cm long by 2–4 cm wide, dark green, ovate-oblong, coarsely crenate. Flowers very pretty, pale purplish blue, large, 3.5–4 cm long, in pairs in upper leaf axils; lateral sepals two, orbicular or ovate-orbicular, 7–8 mm long, lower sepal deeply saccate, 2.5–3.5 cm long, abruptly narrowing into an incurving spur spotted with purple red; dorsal petal kidney-shaped, 2.5–3 cm wide, with dorsal crest; lateral united petals 2.5–3 cm long, upper pair orbicular, 6 mm in diameter, lower pair longer and wider. Seed capsule linear, 3–4 cm long. *Impatiens compta* is only found in Yunnan Province.

Impatiens compta
Yong-Ming Yuan

Impatiens crassicaudex Hooker f.

Erect, robust, much-branched, thick, succulent-stemmed plant, growing to 30 cm in height. Leaves alternate, 3.5 cm long by 1.2 cm wide, ovate, leaf margins crenate. Flowers small, yellow, 1.5 cm long, in pairs at leaf axils or in terminal position; lateral sepals two, narrowly ovate, triangular, lower sepal narrowing to an erect spur, 2–2.5 cm long; dorsal petal orbicular, 8 mm in diameter, with dorsal crest, thickly keeled; lateral united petals 2 cm long, upper pair orbicular, lower pair longer and broader, double the size of upper. Seed capsule linear, 2–2.5 cm long. *Impatiens crassicaudex* is only found in Sichuan and Yunnan Provinces.

Impatiens cristata Wallich

*Impatiens
cyanantha
Yong-Ming Yuan*

Erect, robust, much-branched, annual species, growing to 75 cm in height, sparsely to densely pubescent. Leaves alternate, 5–10 cm long by 2–3.5 cm wide, pubescent, ovate-lanceolate, with two globose basal glands, edges serrate. Flowers golden yellow, 2.5 cm long, in racemes of two to five; lateral sepals two, orbicular, lower sepal saccate, abruptly constricted into a short, narrow, incurving spur; dorsal petal orbicular, with dorsal crest; lateral united petals 2.5 cm long, upper petals orbicular, lower petals longer and broader. Seed capsule linear, 2.5–3 cm long. *Impatiens cristata* is another fairly widespread species, found in China, Bhutan, northern India, and Nepal.

Impatiens cyanantha Hooker f.

A robust, erect, much-branched, annual plant, growing to 60 cm high. Leaves arranged alternately, elliptical to lanceolate, 5–10 cm long by 2–4 cm wide, with two stipitate glands at the base, leaf margins coarsely crenate-serrate. Flowers purplish blue or reddish purple, in racemes of four to six; lateral sepals two, orbicular, leathery, lower sepal saccate, 2.5–3 cm long, elongated into a slender, incurved spur; dorsal petal orbicular, slightly hooded, 7 mm; lateral united petals 2 cm long, upper pair orbicular, small, lower pair larger and broader, narrowing toward the ends. Seed capsule shortly linear or slightly club-shaped, 2.5 cm long. *Impatiens cyanantha* is found growing in southeastern Yunnan Province.

Impatiens cymbifera Hooker f.

An erect, stout, branched, annual species, growing to 1–1.5 m high, stem grooved, often marked with black transverse striping, nodes prominent. Leaves ovate-lanceolate, crenate, 10–13 cm long by 2.5–3.5 cm wide, with two stipular glands at the base of the petiole. Flowers 2.5–3 cm, in racemes of three to six, coming from the axils of the leaves, pale mauve blotched with yellow and some dark purple striping; lateral sepals two, ovate, 1 cm long, lower sepal 15–20 mm long, saccate, dark purple, constricting into a short, straight spur; dorsal petal pale purple, 12 mm long by 20 mm wide, with no dorsal crest; lateral united petals 28–35 mm long, upper lobe very broadly oblong, lower lobe broadly elliptical. Seed capsule linear, about 2 cm long. *Impatiens cymbifera* is found in northern India, Nepal, and Burma.

Impatiens delavayi Franchet

Erect, slender, annual herb, slightly branched, growing to 30–40 cm high. Leaves arranged alternately, broadly ovate or orbicular, margins coarsely crenate, 8–12 cm long by 3.5 cm wide. Flowers purplish red or yellow with

Impatiens cymbifera

*Impatiens
delavayi*
David E. Boufford

purple lower sepal, 2.5–3.5 cm long, in racemes of one to five flowers in leaf axils; lateral sepals two, obliquely ovate or orbicular, lower sepal saccate, abruptly constricted into a short narrow, incurving spur, with dark purple marking along its length; dorsal petal orbicular, slightly hooded, with dorsal crest, pointed at front; lateral united petals 2.5 cm long, upper petals small, orbicular, cupped, lower petals much larger, orbicular, extending to the front. Seed capsule linear, 3–4 cm long, *Impatiens delavayi* is found in Yunnan and Sichuan Provinces. Two color variants are known: the first has purple-red flowers, the other has purple and yellow flowers. Both have very high horticultural merit but are not yet available commercially.

Impatiens dicentra Franchet ex Hooker f.

Erect, much-branched, annual species, growing to 80 cm high. Leaves arranged alternately, 10–15 cm long by 3–7 cm wide, ovate, leaf margins serrate, with pointed teeth. Flowers yellow, single, large, 4 cm long, in axillary position; lateral sepals two, broadly ovate or orbicular, with narrowly keeled midvein, margin coarsely dentate, lower sepal saccate, constricting into an incurving, short, bifid spur; dorsal petal orbicular, 1.5 cm in diameter, with high dorsal keel, lateral petals ovate, tapering into long filamentous hairs. Seed capsule linear, 3 cm long. *Impatiens dicentra* is found in many locations in China, including Guizhou, Henan, and Sichuan.

Impatiens distracta Hooker f.

Erect, slender, annual plant, growing to 50 cm high, branched. Leaves alternate, ovate, membranous and glabrous, margins crenate-serrate. Flowers pink and purple, small, 2 cm, in pairs in upper leaf axils; lateral sepals two, ovate, lower sepal 1.5 cm long, narrowing into a slightly incurved spur; dorsal petal orbicular, 1.4 cm wide, flat, spreading, with dorsal crest; lateral united petals 2–2.5 cm long, upper petals very small, orbicular, lower petals much larger and broader, coming to a point at the bottom, fibrous dorsal auricle hidden inside lower sepal. Seed capsule linear, erect. *Impatiens distracta* is found in Sichuan Province.

Impatiens drepanophora Hooker f.

Tender perennial plant, much branched, growing to 75 cm in height. Leaves arranged alternately, ovate, 5–12 cm long by 2–4 cm wide, edges crenate, petioles 3–5 cm long, with two stipitate glands. Flowers bright yellow, sometimes with some red spotting on the petals, in racemes of five to 10, small, 3 cm long; lateral sepals two, greenish, very small, 2 mm, upturned, lower sepal gradually narrowing into an incurving spur, 2 cm long; dorsal petal orbicular, 7.5 mm across; lateral united petals 2.5 cm long, upper narrowly oblong, lower much longer and slender, coming to a point. Seed capsule linear, 1.5 cm long, dark reddish color. *Impatiens drepanophora* is found in Yunnan Province, India, Nepal, and Sikkim. Although the yellow flowers are quite small, the

Impatiens drepanophora

plant makes up for this by producing a great many in succession throughout the summer months, and so has good garden potential.

Impatiens edgeworthii Hooker f.

A tall, much-branched annual species, with succulent stems, growing to about 1 m high. Leaves arranged alternately, 7–17 cm long by 5 cm wide, ovate, acuminate, with serrated edges, petioled, stipitate glands. Flowers in racemes of three or four, yellow or pale yellow, with some red brown markings in the throat; lateral sepals two, small, ovate, 0.5 cm long, lower sepal 2.5 cm long, funnel-shaped, gradually tapering into a long thin spur, with a slightly swollen tip; dorsal petal orbicular, bilobed, 1.5 cm diameter, with a dorsal crest; lateral united petals 1.5 cm long, lower petal longer than upper. Seed capsule linear, 3–5 cm long. *Impatiens edgeworthii* is generally found in northern India and Kashmir. Normally the flowers are yellow, but there is also a very pale lilac variety.

Impatiens faberi Hooker f.

Erect, branched, perennial species, growing to 50–70 cm high. Leaves arranged alternately, pale green, broadly ovate-elliptical, 5–15 cm long by 2.5–4.5 cm wide, leaf edges serrate or crenate-serrate, petioles 1–1.5 cm long. Flowers purplish red to pale purple, with reddish brown markings, 3–4.5 cm long, usually in pairs, in leaf axils; lateral sepals two, ovate, 6–8 mm long, lower sepal funnel-shaped, narrowing to an incurving spur; dorsal petal orbicular, 1.5 cm wide, dorsal crest, keeled, pointed at front; lateral sepal 2.5 cm long, upper petals orbicular, lower larger. Seed capsule linear, 2.5 cm long. *Impatiens faberi* is only found in the Sichuan Province of China on Mt. Emei.

Impatiens falcifer Hooker f.

Weak, lax or decumbent, annual species, much branched, growing to 50 cm in length. Leaves 3–9 cm long, arranged alternately, shortly petioled or often sessile, ovate, edges sharply serrated, tiny stipular glands. Flowers golden yellow, usually with some red spotting on the dorsal petals, 3–4 cm across; lateral sepals broadly ovate, green, lower sepal funnel-shaped, narrowing into a rather straight, thin spur, 1.5–2.5 cm long; dorsal petal erect, slightly hooded, lateral petals 2.5 cm long, upper petals small and reflexed, lower petals much larger and spreading, falcate or horn-shaped, rounded at the tip. Seed capsule linear, 2.5–5 cm long. *Impatiens falcifer* is usually found in the more easterly areas of the Himalayas from eastern Nepal to Bhutan, usually growing in montane forests.

Impatiens fanjingshanica Y. L. Chen

Lax, procumbent, annual species, growing to 50 cm long, sometimes with purple stems, rooting at the nodes, branched. Leaves alternate, 3–8 cm long by 2–3.5 cm wide, with glands at the base, leaf surface dark green, ovate or ovate-lanceolate, some pubescence along midvein, margin crenate-serrate. Flowers purple, large, 3–4.5 cm, solitary, in upper leaf axils; lateral sepals two, ovate or orbicular, small, lower sepal funnel-shaped, gradually narrowing into an incurving spur, 2–2.5 cm long; dorsal petal orbicular, 1 cm in diameter, emarginated, with dorsal crest, pointed at the front, lateral petals 1.8 cm long, upper pair almost orbicular, lower petals longer and wider, with dorsal auricle. Seed capsule linear. *Impatiens fanjingshanica* is only found in Guizhou Province at Fanjingshan.

Impatiens fenghwaiana Y. L. Chen

Erect, succulent, annual species, growing to 50 cm tall, simple or occasionally branched, rooting at the lower nodes. Leaves arranged alternately, dark

*Impatiens
fenghwaiana*
Yong-Ming Yuan

green, ovate, membranous, margins coarsely crenate. Flowers pink, 3.5 cm long, solitary or sometimes in pairs, in upper leaf axils; lateral sepals two, oblong-ovate, 9 mm, pointed, lower sepal narrowly funnel-shaped, gradually narrowing into an incurving spur, 2.5 cm long; dorsal petal almost orbicular, 1.2 cm by 1.4 cm, shallow dorsal crest, lateral petals 1.7 cm long, upper petals small, oblong-ovate, lower petals longer and wider. Seed capsule linear, 2 cm long. *Impatiens fenghwaiana* is only found in the Jiangxi region.

Impatiens florigeria C. B. Clarke ex Hooker f.

Annual plant growing to 50 cm tall. Leaves arranged alternately, ovate-lanceolate, 4–14 cm long by 1.5–3.5 wide, surface smooth or sometimes slightly pubescent, petioles 1–4 cm long, with stipules at base. Flowers in umbels of two to five, light purple, with lighter colored spur; lower sepal saccate, 1.5 cm long, with short, incurving spur; dorsal petal hooded, 7 mm tall by 8 mm wide, with dorsal crest; lateral united petals 2 cm long, upper pair ovate, lower pair elliptical. Seed capsule spindle-shaped, 1 cm long. *Impatiens florigeria* can be found growing in northern India around Darjeeling and in Bhutan. It will make a very good addition to the garden, producing flowers throughout the summer months.

Impatiens forrestii Hooker ex W. W. Smith

Erect to lax perennial plant, growing to 40–90 cm long, simple to slightly branched, branches slender. Leaves arranged alternately, dark green, ovate to ovate-lanceolate, leaf margins serrate. Flowers purplish red, spotted and lightly streaked in a darker color, in leaf axils, single or in pairs; lateral sepals two, ovate to slightly orbicular, 9 mm by 6 mm, lightly veined, lower sepal saccate, 3 cm long, abruptly narrowing into an incurving spur, 1 cm long; dorsal petal orbicular, 2 cm in diameter, with conspicuous dorsal crest, pointed at front; lateral united petals 3.5 cm long, upper petals almost orbicular, lower petals larger and longer, protruding out at the front. Seed capsule linear, 3 cm long. *Impatiens forrestii* is found in northwestern Yunnan and Sichuan Provinces. This most attractive species has been offered by a few nurseries in Britain and the United States, and it is said to be fairly hardy in most areas.

Impatiens fragicolor Maquand & Airy-Shaw

Erect, succulent, much-branched, annual herb, growing to 60–70 cm high. Leaves arranged alternately, 3–10 cm long by 2–4 cm wide, ovate, leaf margins serrate. Flowers light purple with yellow-ish and red markings, 2.5–3 cm long, in leaf axils, one to five flowers in a raceme; lateral sepals two, ovate, 7.7 mm long, lower sepal funnel-shaped, 2.5 cm long narrowing into an incurving, yellow, slender spur; dorsal petal ovate, 0.75 cm in diameter, slightly emarginated at apex; lateral united petals 2 cm long, upper pair almost ovate, lower pair longer and wider. Seed capsule linear, 2.5–3 cm long. *Impatiens fragicolor* is only found in southwestern China in Yunnan Province. This species is a good garden plant that self-seeds well.

Impatiens fragicolor

Impatiens glandulifera Roylev

Robust, succulent, annual species, growing to 2–3 m high, with thick, hollow stems, strongly branched. Leaves arranged oppositely or in verticils of three

Impatiens candida, a close relative of *I. glandulifera*

or four, 7–12 cm in length, ovate, edges sharply serrated, petiolate, with stipitate glands. Flowers pale pink to dark purple; lateral sepals heart-shaped, lower sepal saccate, 2 cm long, abruptly constricted into a short, incurving spur, 5–6 mm long; dorsal petal orbicular, 2 cm diameter, bilobed, with dorsal crest; lateral united petals 2.6 cm long, unequal in size, lower pair larger than upper. Seed capsule broadly club-shaped, 2–2.5 cm long, seeds globose and 3 mm in diameter. *Impatiens glandulifera* is a very common and widespread plant found in the western Himalayas, Nepal, and Kashmir. This species has become naturalized in many areas in Europe and the United States. The close relative *Impatiens candida* has an identical habit, but with pure white flowers with some yellow coloring in the throat.

Impatiens hunanensis X. L. Chen

Erect, succulent annual species, growing to about 50 cm high, sparsely branched, often rooting at the lower nodes. Leaves arranged alternately, ovate or ovate-lanceolate, 5–15 cm long by 3–4 cm wide, margins coarsely crenate-serrate, petioles 3–4 cm long. Flowers pale to bright yellow, 2.5–3 cm long, usually solitary but sometimes two or three, in upper leaf axils; lateral sepals two, ovate to almost orbicular, thickly textured, lower sepal saccate, 3 cm long, abruptly constricting into an incurving spur; dorsal petal orbicular, 1–1.5 cm diameter, with high, pointed dorsal keel; lateral united petals 2.5 cm long, upper pair orbicular, lower pair larger and wider, prominent dorsal auricle. Seed capsule 3 cm long, club-shaped. *Impatiens hunanensis* is found in Guangdong, Hunnah, and Jiangxi Provinces.

Impatiens infirma Hooker f.

Annual herbs, growing to 60 cm tall, glabrous, stems erect, branched. Leaves arranged alternately, ovate or ovate-lanceolate, 5–13 cm long by 2–3 cm wide, thinly membranous, margins crenate. Flowers yellow, 1.5–2 cm wide, in racemes of a few to more than 10, in upper leaf axils; lateral sepals two, obliquely ovate, 3 mm long, lower sepal boat-shaped, base narrowing into an incurved or involute spur, 2 cm long; dorsal petal obovate-orbicular, cup-shaped, with dorsal crest; lateral united petals 1.5 cm long, upper pair broadly orbicular, lower pair dolabriform. Seed capsule narrowly fusiform, 1.5–2 cm long. *Impatiens infirma* can be found in Sichuan Province and Tibet.

Impatiens insignis DC

Perennial herb, upright, growing to about 1 m in height, few branches, sometimes rooting at the lower nodes, stems angular. Leaves sessile or subsessile, 5–9 cm long by 2 cm wide, elliptic-lanceolate, margins shallowly crenate to serrate, finely pubescent on both sides, dark green above pale green below. Flowers in terminal racemes of three or four; lateral sepals ovate, 6 mm by 3 mm, lower sepal funnel-shaped, narrowing into a long thin spur, 2–5 cm long, slightly upturned; dorsal petal ovate, slightly recurving at apex, 0.5 cm wide by 1 cm long; lateral united petals 1.5 cm long, upper 1 cm long by 0.5 cm wide, lower oblong, 1 cm long. Seed capsules 1 cm long. *Impatiens insignis* is only found in northern India in the eastern Himalayas.

Impatiens insignis

Impatiens lateristachys Y. L. Chen & Y. Q. Lu

A much-branched, erect, annual herb, growing to 1 m in height. Leaves arranged alternately, 6 cm long by 1–1.5 cm wide, with stipitate glands at the base, both surfaces slightly hairy, edges serrate. Flowers red, pink, or white, in racemes of three to five in leaf axils, 3 cm by 2 cm; lateral sepals two, subulate, 2 mm long, lower sepal horn-shaped, 2.5–3 cm long, with an erect, strong spur; dorsal petal almost orbicular, 1.5–1.8 cm wide, emarginated at the top, shallow dorsal keel; lateral united petals 2.5–3 cm long, upper petals orbicular, lower longer and wider, with linear dorsal auricle inserted into the spur. Seed capsule linear, 3 cm long. *Impatiens lateristachys* is mainly found in the Sichuan Province of China, on Mt. Emei.

Impatiens lecomtei Hooker f.

Erect annual herb, growing to 50 cm in height, simple or sparsely branched. Leaves alternate, ovate to ovate-lanceolate, 10–15 cm long by 2.5–3 cm wide, membranous, margins coarsely crenate. Flowers pink, large, 3.5–4 cm long, single, in upper leaf axils; lateral sepals two, orbicular, 1–1.5 cm in diameter, membranous, lower sepal 3–3.5 cm long, funnel-shaped, with violet striping, gradually narrowing into an incurved, slender, bifid spur; dorsal petal orbic-

Impatiens lecomtei
Yong-Ming Yuan

ular, 2 cm in diameter, with dorsal crest; lateral united petals 3–3.5 cm long, upper pair small, ovate, coming to a fine point, lower petals much larger and wider, with elongated dorsal auricle. Seed capsule linear, 2.5–3 cm long. *Impatiens lecomtei* is only found in northwestern Yunnan Province.

Impatiens lingzhiensis Y. L. Chen

Simple to sparsely branched species, growing to 60 cm high. Leaves arranged alternately, 5–13 cm long by 1–1.5 cm wide, with a pair of stipitate glands near the base, linear-lanceolate, margins sharply serrate, petioles 1.5 cm long. Flowers pale purple, 4 cm long, in pairs at leaf axils; lateral sepals four, outer pair falcate, inner linear, with tailed extension, lower sepal saccate, gradually narrowing into a hooked, incurving spur; dorsal petal hooded, orbicular, with dorsal keel, lateral petals 2 cm long, upper pair ovate, lower petals oblong. Seed capsule linear, 3 cm long. *Impatiens lingzhiensis* is only found in the Lingzhi area of China.

Impatiens macrovexilla Y. L. Chen

An erect, succulent, annual species, growing to 30 cm high, few branches, tending to lose lower leaves. Leaves arranged alternately, dark green, oblong, or oblong-lanceolate, 5–10 cm long by 2.5–4 cm wide, thinly textured, often with two globose glands at base, leaf edges crenate. Flowers purple, 3–4 cm long, in pairs in leaf axils; lateral sepals two, green, broadly ovate, 5–6 mm, lower sepal narrowly funnel-shaped, 4–4.5 cm long, gradually narrowing into a slender, incurving spur, 2 cm long; dorsal petal kidney-shaped, large, 1.5 cm long by 3.5 cm wide, with dorsal crest, lateral petals 2.5 cm long, upper pair oblong, rounded at the tip, lower petals longer and broader, slightly triangular. Seed capsule linear, 1.8–2 cm long. *Impatiens macrovexilla* is only found in Yunnan Province.

Impatiens margaritifera Hooker f.

Erect annual herb, growing to 40–50 cm tall, stem branched or simple. Leaves alternate or opposite, alternate below and changing to opposite toward middle, 3–10 cm long by 1.5–3.5 cm wide, membranous, with two large basal glands, margins coarsely crenate, petioles 1.5 cm long. Flowers white, small, 2 cm, in axillary racemes of six to eight; lateral sepals two, ovate, orbicular, small, pointed, lower sepal boat-shaped, with no spur; dorsal petal elliptical-obovate or suborbicular, with slight dorsal crest, pointed at the top; lateral united petals 1.5 cm, upper pair ovate-oblong or suborbicular, lower petals narrowly dolabriform or oblong dolabriform. Seed capsule linear, 1–2 cm long. *Impatiens margaritifera* is found in southwestern Sichuan and Yunnan Provinces and Tibet.

Impatiens marianae Reichenbach f. ex Hooker f.

Erect or trailing herb, growing to about 1 m long, rooting at the nodes, pubescent in all parts. Leaves alternate, ovate, margins shallowly serrate, 5–10 cm long by 2–5 cm wide, papillose-hairy, with pronounced variegated patterning, petioles 1–1.5 cm long. Flowers purple, solitary, 1–2.5 cm long; lateral sepals two, small, ovate, lower sepal slightly pouched, 2.5–3 cm long, gradually constricted into a thin spur, 1.2 cm long; dorsal petal small, hooded; lateral united petals 2 cm long, upper pair triangular, lower pair almost orbicu-

Impatiens marianae

lar. Seed capsule spindle-shaped, turgid at the center, 0.5 cm long. *Impatiens marianae* is only found in the states of Assam and Meghalaya in India.

Impatiens mengtzeana Hooker f.

Lax or somewhat trailing, sometimes upright, perennial plant, growing to 50 cm long, often rooting at the nodes. Leaves arranged alternately, 5–10 cm long by 2.5–5 cm wide, elliptical to oblanceolate, dark green, edges crenate-serrate, petioles 2.5–3 cm long. Flowers usually yellow but can be orange, pink, or white, large, 3–5 cm long, in leaf axils, single or in pairs; lateral sepals two, ovate, 6–8 mm by 6 mm, lower sepal usually lightly spotted, funnel-shaped narrowing into a long, involute spur, 2.5 cm long; dorsal petal orbicular, 1.5–1.8 cm across, with slight dorsal crest; lateral united petals 2 cm long, upper pair orbicular, lower pair longer and broader. Seed capsule linear-oblong, 1.5–2.5 cm long. *Impatiens mengtzeana* is another widespread species found growing in Thailand and in southwestern China.

Impatiens mengtzeana, orange form

Impatiens monticola Hooker f.

A robust, succulent, annual species, with few branches, growing to 50 cm high. Leaves alternate, 5–13 cm long by 3–4.5 cm wide, obovate or ovate-elliptical, margins crenate, petioles 3–4 cm long. Flowers white to pale yellow, 3.5 cm long, in pairs in upper leaf axils; lateral sepals two, green, ovate to orbicular, 8 mm by 8–10 mm long, lower sepal yellow with some orange streaking, 1.8 cm long narrowing into an involute spur; dorsal petal orbicular, 2 cm in diameter, with dorsal crest; lateral united petals 2–2.5 cm long, upper pair small, almost orbicular, lower pair longer and wider. Seed capsule erect, narrowly spindle-shaped. *Impatiens monticola* is only found in Sichuan Province.

Impatiens morsei Hooker f.

An erect, branched, succulent plant, growing to 30–40 cm in height, stems fleshy, purple tinged. Leaves dark, velvety green, with pinkish red midvein, ovate, 8–13 long by 4–7 cm wide, with two globose glands at the base, margins crenate-serrulate. Flowers inflated, white, light pink, or pale purple, heavily

*Impatiens
morsei*

spotted with orange inside the throat, 3–3.5 cm long; lateral sepals two, green, ovate, 1 cm, pronounced midvein, pointed, lower sepal pouched, 2 cm long, abruptly constricted into an incurving forked spur; dorsal petal 1–1.5 cm wide, bilobed, with dorsal crest, lateral petals 2–3 cm long, upper petals falcate, lower oblong protruding to the front. Seed capsule club-shaped, 2 cm long. *Impatiens morsei* is only found in the Guangxi area of China. Selected clones of this plant have been offered in garden centers and nurseries worldwide for some time, sold under the names *Impatiens morsei* 'Velvetea' or *I. morsei* 'Secret Love'. This species is a particularly beautiful plant that can be ideal for growing as a flowering houseplant.

Impatiens namchabarwensis R. J. Morgan, Y. M. Yuan & X. J. Ge

Glabrous perennial species, growing to 40–50 cm high, much branched, with narrow stems, slightly woody at base, lower stems rooting at nodes. Leaves arranged alternately, 6–8 cm long by 3–4 cm wide, ovate, margins shallowly serrated, petiolate, with single gland at each side of leaf base, flat stipules at nodes. Flowers in pairs at leaf axils, bright ultramarine blue, with central white patch and yellow eye; sepals four, upper small and linear, lower larger and ovate, lower sepal 2.5–3 cm long, funnel-shaped, gradually narrowing into an upturned and incurving, slender spur; dorsal petal orbicular, 1.5 cm,

Impatiens namchabarwensis

prominent, forward-pointing dorsal keel; lateral united petals 2–2.5 cm long, upper ovate, 1.5 cm by 1 cm, lower larger, oblong, 2 cm by 1 cm, with small dorsal auricle, curling forward. Seed capsule linear, 3–4 cm. *Impatiens namchabarwensis* is only found in Tibet and is the only known blue-flowered species. The species is self-seeding and very floriferous, flowering throughout the summer months. *Impatiens namchabarwensis* is destined to become a great addition to the summer garden, although it is half-hardy in most areas.

Impatiens noli-tangere Linnaeus

An erect, many-branched, succulent, annual plant, growing to about 1 m in height. Leaves arranged alternately, slightly glaucous, ovate, edges widely crenate, petioles 2–5 cm long. Flowers yellow, in an inflorescence of two to four; lateral sepals two, broadly ovate, 5–6 mm, lower sepal with some orange spotting inside the throat, funnel-shaped, narrowing into a thin incurving spur, 1–1.5 cm long; dorsal petal orbicular, 1 cm in diameter with emarginated apex, green dorsal crest; lateral united petals 2–2.5 cm long, upper petals small, oblong, lower petals longer. Seed capsule linear, 2–2.5 cm long. *Impatiens noli-tangere* is probably the most widespread species in the genus. It is indigenous to Britain and is found in places across Europe and throughout Asia, even as far east as Japan and Korea. It is the only *Impatiens* species

*Impatiens
omeiana*

native to Great Britain. *Impatiens noli-tangere* has been used as a garden plant for many years; although it self-seeds with ease, it is quite easy to control. It was one of the first *Impatiens* species described by Linnaeus.

Impatiens omeiana Hooker f.

Erect perennial plant growing from robust, slightly tuberous rhizomes, stems simple, unbranched, growing to 30–50 cm high. Leaves arranged alternately, oblong ovate or sometimes lanceolate, 15–20 cm long by 4–6 cm wide, leaf edges coarsely crenate, dark green with pale yellow to cream herringbone patterning along center vein. Flowers in terminal racemes of four or five, yellow, flushed orange, large, 3.5–4.5 cm long; lateral sepals four, lower pair obliquely ovate, upper pair horn-shaped, lower sepal long, saccate, abruptly constricted into a narrow, involute, short spur; dorsal petal orbicular, hooded, with thin dorsal crest; lateral united petals 2.5 cm long, upper petals half the size of the lower, which protrude out at the front. Seed capsule linear, 3 cm long. *Impatiens omeiana* is only found growing on Mt. Emei in Sichuan Province. Two unnamed varieties are known. Variety 1 lacks the central marking of the leaf and has very pale, cream-colored flowers. Variety 2 lacks the central leaf marking and has pale yellow flowers.

Impatiens oxyanthera

Impatiens oxyanthera Hooker f.

Perennial herb, erect, simple stemmed, growing to 40 cm tall. Leaves arranged alternately, 6–8 cm long by 3.5–4 cm wide, ovate, dark green, margins coarsely serrate, with pointed teeth. Flowers red or purplish red, 2–2.5 cm long, in pairs, in upper leaf axils; lateral sepals orbicular, 5 mm in diameter, lower sepal funnel-shaped, 2.5 cm long, narrowing into an incurving spur, with some red striping; dorsal petal orbicular, 1.5 cm in diameter, with dorsal keel, pointed at the front; lateral united petals 2–2.5 cm long, upper petals orbicular, lower petals longer, curved narrowly falcate. Seed capsule linear. *Impatiens oxyanthera* is only found in Sichuan Province.

Impatiens parviflora DC

Annual herb, smooth stem and leaves, erect with some branching, growing to 30–60 cm high. Leaves alternate, petioles 1.5–2 cm long, ovate, 6–10 cm long by 4–5 cm wide, thin texture, leaf edges acutely serrate. Flowers in inflorescence of four to 20 small, 1-cm long, pale yellow blooms, sometimes with some red striping in the throat, sepals two, ovate, very small, lower sepal funnel-shaped, abruptly narrowing into a thin spur, 7 mm long; dorsal petal orbicular, 5 mm in diameter; lateral united petals 1 cm long, upper petals ovate, lower elongated, bilobed. Seed capsule linear, 2–2.5 cm long. *Impatiens parviflora* is an extremely widespread species found in many locations from northern India through to Russia and most central Asian countries. It has become naturalized in many parts of Europe, including Britain. *Impatiens parviflora*, however,is not of sufficient floral interest to be of much use in the garden.

Impatiens platychlaena Hooker f.

Tall, erect, much-branched, annual plant, growing to about 1 m in height. Leaves arranged alternately, ovate-lanceolate, 5–15 cm long by 3–4.5 cm wide, leaf margins coarsely crenate-serrate. Flowers large, 3–4 cm long, bicolored, in pairs in terminal position; lateral sepals brown or dark purple, orbicular, 1.5 cm wide, lower sepal deeply saccate, 2.5–3 cm long, abruptly constricted into an incurving, stout, bifurcate spur; dorsal petal purple or yellow, orbicular, 1.5 cm in diameter, pointed at the center, with dorsal crest; lateral united petals 2.5–3 cm long, upper pair orbicular with extended filamentous hairs, lower petals longer and broader, also with extended hairs. Seed capsule linear, 2.5 cm long. *Impatiens platychlaena* is a common species in the Sichuan Province of China.

Impatiens pritzelii Hooker f.

Impatiens pritzelii

Perennial species growing to 50 cm in height, succulent stem, rhizomatous, slightly decumbent, simple. Leaves arranged alternately, sessile, oblong-lanceolate or elliptical, 6–12 cm long by 2–5 cm wide, margins crenate. Flowers yellow to orange, in upper leaf axils, in long racemes of three to six flowers, 2–2.5 cm long; lateral sepals four, upper pair ovate, 8 mm by 5 mm, lower lanceolate, lower sepal saccate, gradually narrowing into an incurving, involute spur; dorsal petal ovate, 11.5 cm wide; lateral united petals 2 cm, upper pair ovate, lower longer and wider, with reflexed dorsal auricle. Seed capsule linear, 3 cm long. *Impatiens pritzelii* is only found in Yunnan and Sichuan Provinces.

Impatiens puberula DC

Scrambling, weakly branched, perennial plant, growing to 20–50 cm in length. Leaves arranged alternately, rather setose, petioled, ovate, 6–15 cm long by 2–5 cm wide, leaf margins roughly crenate. Flowers solitary, in leaf axils, purplish blue, 2.5–3 cm across; lateral sepals almost orbicular, 6 mm long, lower sepal white to pale pink, funnel-shaped, gradually tapering into long spur, 2 cm in length; dorsal petal widely ovate, 15 cm long by 2 cm wide, apex slightly emarginated, with a dorsal keel; lateral united petals 20–22 mm long, upper lobe small, almost orbicular, lower lobe much larger, almost elliptical. Seed capsule 2 cm long, spindle-shaped. *Impatiens puberula* is a common plant in northern India and Nepal.

Impatiens racemosa DC

Well-branched annual, growing to 20–60 cm high. Leaves dark reddish tinged, arranged alternately, broadly lanceolate, 4–10 cm long by 1–2.5 cm wide, smooth surfaces, leaf edges crenate. Flowers in racemes of three to six, in leaf axils, bright yellow, 2–3 cm long; lateral sepals two, 2–3 mm long, ovate, lower sepal funnel-shaped, tapering into a thin, curved spur, 2 cm in length; dorsal petal 3 cm by 5 cm, hooded, with no dorsal crest; lateral united petals, 10–18 mm long, upper ovate, 3 mm long, lower petal 10–15 mm long.

*Impatiens
racemosa*

Seed capsule linear, thin, 1.5–2 cm long. *Impatiens racemosa* is a common plant of northern India and Nepal.

Impatiens radiata Hooker f.

Slender, many-branched, erect, annual species, growing to 60 cm tall. Leaves arranged alternately, ovate lanceolate, 6–12 cm long by 2–3 cm wide, darkish green, petioles 1.5–2.5 cm long, leaf margins crenate. Flowers in many-flowered 15-cm-long whorls or sprays, in upper leaf axils, small, about 1 cm long, pale pink, sometimes yellowish; lateral sepals ovate, minute, lower sepal small tapering into an erect, short spur; dorsal petal almost orbicular, 5 mm in diameter; lateral united petals small, oblong, elongated. Seed capsule linear, 2.5 cm long, dark red. *Impatiens radiata* is another widespread species, found growing in Sichuan and Yunnan Provinces, Bhutan, India, Nepal, and Sikkim. It is a species with only minimal horticultural potential.

Impatiens rectangula Handel-Mazzetti

An erect annual herb, growing to 30–70 cm in height, glabrous, branched. Leaves arranged alternately, crowded near the top, ovate or ovate-lanceolate, 4–17 cm long by 2.5–5 cm wide, dark green above, sparsely brownish pilose below, almost sessile above, petiolate below, petioles 4.5 cm long, membranous with stipitate glands, margins densely crenate. Flowers sulfur yellow, 1.5–2 cm long, in many-flowered terminal racemes; lateral sepals two, green, obliquely ovate or almost S-shaped, 2–4 mm long, lower sepal boat-shaped, 8 mm, gradually narrowing into a rectangular spur, 3.5 cm long; dorsal petal almost four-sided to orbicular, 6 mm in diameter; lateral united petals 2–10 mm long, upper petals orbicular, short, lower petals narrowly dolabriform, twice the size of the upper. Seed capsule fusiform, 2.5–3 cm long. *Impatiens rectangula* is found along the margins of bamboo forests in northwestern Yunnan Province.

Impatiens rhombifolia Y. Q. Lu & Y. L. Chen

Prostrate or trailing, perennial herb, growing to 30–40 cm long. Leaves arranged alternately, rhombic to almost rhombic in shape, 2.5 cm long by 1.5 cm wide, with few stipitate glands, margins serrate. Flowers bright yellow, 2 cm wide, in pairs at leaf axils; lateral sepals two, yellowish green, small, ovate to orbicular, lower sepal 2 cm, abruptly constricted into a thin, long, erect spur, 2 cm long; dorsal petal orbicular, 2 cm in diameter, slightly bilobed;

Impatiens rhombifolia

lateral united petals 2 cm long, upper petals small, sometimes red spotted, lower petals longer and broader. Seed capsule linear, 2 cm long. *Impatiens rhombifolia* is only found in the Sichuan Province of China on Mt. Emei.

Impatiens rubrostriata Hooker f.

Impatiens rubrostriata Yong-Ming Yuan

Erect, succulent, branched annual plant, growing to 30–90 cm high. Leaves arranged alternately, ovate or elliptical, 5–10 cm long by 3–6 cm wide, with some basal glands. Flowers white with red striping inside and outside, large, 4–5 cm long, in racemes of four or five; lateral sepals very small, green, lower sepals deeply saccate, 3 cm long, abruptly constricting into a very incurving slender spur; dorsal petal orbicular, heavily hooded, 1.5 cm in diameter, with pronounced dorsal keel, lateral petals 1–1.5 cm, upper petals orbicular-elliptical, lower petals longer and wider. Seed capsule spindular, 2.5 cm long. *Impatiens rubrostriata* is mainly found in Yunnan Province.

Impatiens ruiliensis S. Akiyama & H. Ohba

Erect annual herb, growing to 40–60 cm tall, stem purple tinged, branched. Leaves arranged alternately, broadly elliptical to ovate, 7–13 cm long by 3–6 cm wide, with one or two pairs of stipitate basal glands, glabrous, margins crenate, petiolate. Flowers white to yellowish, small, 1.5–2 cm; lateral sepals two, falcate-elliptical, 2 mm, lower sepal navicular, base narrowing into an erect or curved spur, 3 cm long, slender; dorsal petal obovate, slightly cupped, 8 mm by 6 mm, with dorsal crest, lateral petals yellowish, spotted red at the base, 1.8 mm long, upper petals triangular, 9 mm long, lower petals curved and lanceolate. Seed capsule linear, 3–4 cm long. *Impatiens ruiliensis* is only found in western Yunnan Province.

Impatiens scabrida DC

Impatiens scabrida

Annual herb growing to 60–120 cm high, thick stem, erect, much branched. Leaves alternate, obscurely pubescent, 10–15 cm long by 4–6 cm wide, ovate, margins serrated, large kidney-shaped gland at one side of the base of petiole, smaller, spherical gland on the other side. Flowers yellow or pale yellow in racemes of two to five, large, 3.5 cm long; lateral sepals two, small, ovate,

pale greenish brown, lower sepal large, 3–3.5 cm long, constricting into a thin, curving spur, saccate, pale yellow, with reddish brown markings in the throat; dorsal petal large, orbicular, 1.5–2 cm diameter, with keeled dorsal crest; lateral united petals 2.2 cm long, upper broadly obovate, 1 cm diameter, lower narrowly oblong, 1–1.2 cm long. Seed capsule linear, 3.5–5 cm long. *Impatiens scabrida* is found in many locations in the Himalayas, northern India, Kashmir, Himashal Pradesh, Uttar Pradesh, western Bengal, Sikkim, Nepal, and Pakistan. It is a quite variable species in color and habit.

Impatiens siculifer Hooker f.

Slender annual herb, with few branches, growing to 50 cm high. Leaves arranged alternately, elliptical or ovate-lanceolate, 5–15 cm long by 2.5–5 cm wide, leaf margins coarsely crenate. Flowers yellow or purple, 3 cm long, in racemes of five or six, in upper leaf axils; lateral sepals two, narrowly oblong, 5 mm long, lower sepal narrowly funnel-shaped, tapering into a long incurving or recurving spur, 2–3 cm long; dorsal petal almost orbicular with narrow dorsal crest; lateral united petals 1–2 cm long, upper petals triangular, lower longer and drawn out into thin filaments. Seed capsule club-shaped. *Impatiens siculifer* is a fairly widespread species in China, found growing in many places including Sichuan and Yunnan Provinces.

Impatiens soulieana Hooker f.

An upright, branched, slender, annual species, growing to 40–50 cm high. Leaves arranged alternately, 5–9 cm long by 2.5–3 cm wide, coarsely crenate, petioles 1.5 cm long. Flowers lemon yellow, with red or purple striping in the throat, 2.5–3 cm long; lateral sepals two, broadly ovate, 1 cm in length, lower sepal funnel-shaped, 2.5–3 cm long, base gradually narrowing into an incurving, clavate spur; dorsal petal orbicular, 2–2.2 cm in diameter, with thin dorsal crest, lateral petals 2.5 cm long, lower petals ovate, pointed, lower petals longer and wider. Seed capsule linear, 2.5–3 cm long. *Impatiens soulieana* is another Sichuan species, found in forests near rivers or streams. Two flower types are known in this species, with the second

Impatiens soulieana

being much paler. *Impatiens soulieana* has been offered by a few nurseries and makes a very fine addition to garden borders; it self-seeds well.

Impatiens stenantha Hooker f.

Upright, much-branched, perennial plant, growing to 30–60 cm high. Leaves arranged alternately, dark reddish green, elliptical-ovate, 12–15 cm long by 3–5 cm wide, leaf edges coarsely crenate, petioles 1–3.5 cm long. Flowers in inflorescence of three to five, axillary or terminal, bright yellow or with some dark red to brown spotting; lateral sepals two, small lanceolate, 4 mm long, lower sepal funnel-shaped, tapering into a narrow, upturned spur, 2.5 cm long; dorsal petal orbicular, 1 cm long; lateral united petals 2 cm long, upper pair ovate, lower petals long and narrow. Seed capsule linear, 2–2.5 cm long. *Impatiens stenantha* is a fairly widespread species found in northern India, Sikkim, Nepal, and Yunnan. It has been offered by a few nurseries recently. This species makes a fine garden plant and appears to be quite hardy.

Impatiens sulcata Wallich

An erect, robust, annual species, growing to 2 m in height, branched in the upper portion. Leaves opposite or whorled, elliptical-ovate, 6–20 cm long

*Impatiens
stenantha*

by 2–4.5 cm wide, with some red or purple stipitate glands at the base, leaf edges crenate-serrate. Flowers large, pink, 2.5–3 cm long, in many-flowered racemes; lateral sepals two, ovate, pointed, lower sepal saccate, abruptly narrowing into an incurving spur, 4–5 mm long; dorsal petal almost orbicular, 1.5 cm; lateral united petals wide, upper petals smaller than the lower. Seed capsule club-shaped, 2.5 cm long. *Impatiens sulcata* is fairly widespread in southern China, Bhutan, northern India, Kashmir, and Sikkim.

Impatiens tenuibracteata Y. L. Chen

Erect, slender, little-branched annual species, growing to 50 cm in height. Leaves arranged alternately, ovate or ovate-lanceolate, 2.5–8 cm long by 2–3.5 cm wide, leaf margins coarsely crenate. Flowers purple, 2 cm long, in leaf axils in racemes of six to 10, held above foliage; lateral sepals two, ovate, pointed, 5 mm long, lower sepal purple spotted, narrowly funnel-shaped, tapering into a long, curved, involute spur; dorsal petal orbicular, 6 mm in diameter, with

Impatiens tenuibracteata
Yong-Ming Yuan

dorsal crest, pointed at front; lateral united petals 2 cm long, upper petals almost ovate, lower petals much longer and narrower. Seed capsule linear, 2 cm long. *Impatiens tenuibracteata* comes from the Medog region of Tibet.

Impatiens thomsonii Hooker f.

Erect annual herb, growing to 15–30 cm high, stem simple or branched above, slightly four-angled, glabrous. Leaves alternate, or sometimes in verticils, lower leaves petiolate, upper leaves sessile, ovate-lanceolate, 6–12 cm long by 3–4 cm wide, with two globose stipitate glands at the base of the petiole, both surfaces glabrous, margins crenate-serrate. Flowers pale rose, in few-flowered racemes in upper leaf axils, 1–2 cm long; lateral sepals two, green, obliquely ovate, pointed, lower sepal broadly funnel-shaped, abruptly narrowed into a slender, incurving spur; dorsal petal orbicular pointed at the apex; lateral united petals 1.2–1.5 cm long, upper petals yellow with red spots, oblong, lower petals deep pink, dolabriform. Seed capsule club-shaped, five-angled, 2.5 cm long. *Impatiens thomsonii* is a fairly widespread species found in north-western India, Kashmir, Burma, Sikkim, and Tibet.

Impatiens tortisepala Hooker f.

Erect, much-branched, annual species, slender, growing to 40–50 cm high. Leaves arranged alternately, 10–15 cm long by 3–6 cm wide, ovate to oblong, dark green, thinly textured, margins crenate, petioles 1 cm long. Flowers yellow, with two red spots in the throat, with some red marking on the lower sepal, flowers in racemes of one to five, in leaf axils; lateral sepals two, orbicular, slightly twisted, 5 mm long, lower sepal 2.5 cm long, saccate, narrowing and constricting into a narrow strongly incurving or twisted spur, 1.5 cm long; dorsal petal kidney-shaped, 1.5 cm across, with green dorsal keel; lateral united petals 2–2.5 cm long, upper small and orbicular, lower wider and rounded. Seed capsule linear, 3–4 cm long. *Impatiens tortisepala* is only found in the Sichuan Province of China.

Impatiens trichosepala Y. L. Chen

Small, erect, or somewhat creeping, succulent plant, few branches, growing to 15–25 cm high. Leaves arranged spirally, often crowded near the top, dark green, narrowly lanceolate or oblanceolate, 3.5 cm long by 1–2 cm wide, with two or three glands near base, some yellow brown pubescence along undersides of leaves, leaf edges crenate-serrate, teeth curved. Flowers solitary, in leaf axils, yellow, large, 4–4.5 cm long; lateral sepals two, ovate, 1 cm long by 6 mm wide, with many fine hairs at edges, pointed, lower sepal broadly funnel-shaped, gradually narrowing into an incurved spur; dorsal petal heavily hooded, orbicular, 1.2 cm in diameter, emarginate at the top, dorsal crest highly keeled, slightly pubescent; lateral united petals 2.2 cm long, basal petals almost orbicular, lower petals wider. Seed capsule linear, 3 cm long. *Impatiens trichosepala* is found in Guangxi and Guizhou Provinces in China.

Impatiens uliginosa Franchet

An erect, robust, annual species, growing to 60–70 cm tall. Leaves arranged alternately, dark green, narrowly lanceolate. Flowers red, 2.5–3 cm long, in racemes of three to five, in leaf axils; lateral sepals two, obliquely ovate or orbicular, lower sepal funnel-shaped, 1.5 cm long, narrowing to an incurving spur; dorsal petal orbicular, 1–1.2 cm in diameter, with dorsal crest; lateral united petals 1.5 cm long, upper pair orbicular, lower pair longer, twice the size. Seed capsule linear, 3 cm long. *Impatiens uliginosa* is only found in Yunnan Province.

Impatiens undulata Y. L. Chen & Y. Q. Lu

Erect annual species growing to about 1 m in height, glabrous, much branched. Leaves alternate, sessile above, light green, ovate, 2–5 cm long by 2–4 cm wide, margins undulate or obscurely crenate. Flowers yellow, 2 cm long, in racemes of one to three, in leaf axils; lateral sepals two, small, ovate or orbicular, lower sepal cup-shaped, 2–3 cm long, narrowing into slender involute spur; dorsal petal almost orbicular, 5 mm, with dorsal keel; lateral united petals 1.2 cm long, upper pair small, lower larger and longer with dorsal auricle. Seed capsule fusiform, 1.5–2 cm long, black. *Impatiens undulata* is found in Sichuan Province on Mt. Emei.

Impatiens urticifolia Wallich

Slender, branched, perennial herb, growing to 50–70 cm high. Leaves arranged alternately, elliptical-ovate, 8–20 cm long by 2.5–6 cm wide, membranous, leaf edges crenate. Flowers 2.5 cm long, in axillary racemes of three to five, yellow or pale purple, with darker reddish markings; lateral sepals two, obliquely ovate, lower sepal shortly saccate, abruptly narrowing into a short, incurving spur; dorsal petal orbicular, with narrow dorsal crest; lateral united petals 2 cm long, upper pair orbicular, lower pair longer, elongating to a point. Seed capsule linear, 2.5 cm long. *Impatiens urticifolia* is found growing in many places, including Bhutan, Nepal, and Sikkim.

Impatiens waldheimiana Hooker f.

An erect, perennial herb, growing to 50 cm tall, branched, glabrous. Leaves alternate, 6–10 cm long, ovate, membranous, often with stipitate glands at the base, margins coarsely crenate-serrate, petiole 3.5 cm long. Flowers pale yellow and white, 4 cm long, in pairs in upper leaf axils; lateral sepals two, ovate, 1.5 cm long, base caudate, midvein thickened and keeled, lower sepal broadly funnel-shaped, 2.5 cm long, gradually narrowing into an incurving, bilobed spur; dorsal petal orbicular, 2.2 cm long, with dorsal crest; lateral united petals 3 cm long, upper petals pressed inward, lower petals ovate, apex acuminate, with long filamentous hairs. Seed capsule unknown. *Impatiens waldheimiana* is found in western Sichuan.

Impatiens xanthina H. F. Comber

Impatiens xanthina
Yong-Ming Yuan

A small, low-growing annual or sometimes perennial plant, growing to 6–20 cm high, simple or slightly branched. Leaves arranged alternately, dark green, crowded near the growing tip, petiole 1.5 cm long, lanceolate or elliptical-lanceolate, leaf margin crenate to serrate, 5–7 cm long by 2 cm wide. Flowers golden yellow, spotted dark purplish brown at the center, single or in pairs, 2.5 cm across, flat; lateral sepals two, ovate, 9 mm, lower sepal funnel-shaped, gradually narrowing into an incurving spur, 2.5 cm long; dorsal petal almost orbicular, 6–7 mm in diameter, slightly hairy behind; lateral united petals 1.5–2 cm long, upper petals small, orbicular, lower larger and wider. Seed capsule spindle-shaped, 1 cm long. *Impatiens xanthina* is only found in very humid places in northwestern Yunnan Province.

Impatiens yingjiangensis S. Akiyama & H. Ohba

Lax perennial herb, simple stem with few branches, growing to 40–70 cm in height. Leaves alternate, dark green, elliptical to ovate, 7–15 cm long by 2.5–5 cm wide, with one or two pairs of stipitate glands near the base, edges shallowly crenate. Flowers 3 cm, pink to red, in upper leaf axils usually in pairs; lateral sepals two, orbicular, 8 mm, pointed, lower sepal pink with some yellow, 2.4 cm long, abruptly constricted into a thin, involute spur; dorsal petal pink, broadly ovate, 2 cm long by 2.2 cm wide, dorsally keeled; lateral united petals 3.8 cm long, upper petals broadly oblong, lower petals ovate, rounded. Seed capsule linear, 2.5–3 cm long. *Impatiens yingjiangensis* is mainly found growing in western Yunnan Province.

10

Impatiens of Southern India and Sri Lanka

For many years it was assumed that the ancestral home of the genus *Impatiens* was southern India, an area from which it gradually spread to all other centers of development, migrating northward toward the Himalayas, east to Thailand and Malaysia, and west to Africa and Madagascar. Recent studies in plant phylogeny, however, have called the theory into question, pointing the direction toward the region including Thailand, Malaysia, Cambodia, and Vietnam. Whatever the origins, India has some of the most diverse forms of *Impatiens* in the world.

The southwestern part of the Indian subcontinent, particularly the western Ghats, a chain of mountains stretching some 600 km from Karnataka in the north, through Tamil Nadu, and south to Kerala, is home to the highest concentration of *Impatiens* species in the world. Almost all of these species are endemic to the area, many to individual mountain locations. Once very rich in animal and plant species, much of the area has been taken over for agriculture, particularly the production of tea and coffee. Some forest areas remain, however, and in many cases these *sholas* have become the last refuge for some endemic species. Although the area was well studied by botanists throughout the 19th and 20th centuries, few of its *Impatiens* species are known to Western horticulture, which seems a pity as so many of these plants would make excellent additions to the gardens of Europe and North America.

Like many other tropical regions where *Impatiens* species are found, temperatures are far too high at lower elevations for sustainable growth. The species are almost always found at high elevations, where temperatures are similar to

Opposite: Indian tea plantation

those in more temperate climates. Therefore, most of the southern Indian and Sri Lankan *Impatiens* species would transfer quite well to Western gardens.

The climatic conditions of southern India depends on the effects of two major monsoon periods interspersed with very long dry seasons, which effectively determines the length of the growing period of many of these species. Some high-elevation species manage to cope with these extremes by growing near rivers or streams or otherwise boggy ground, whereas others, both annual and perennial species, adapt by having a very short growing season. After the long dry periods are broken by rains of the first, southwesterly monsoon, usually arriving in late June, most *Impatiens* species are stirred into growth. Some will keep growing until the end of the second, northeasterly monsoon, after which nearly all close down for the rest of the year.

Indian impatiens show a particularly high degree of variation, so much so that they have been placed into three distinct groups. First, the scapigerous, are stemless, usually rosette-forming species; the leaves and flower scapes arise directly from tuberous corms, to which they die back to at the end of the growing season. This feature is unique to Indian *Impatiens* species. Second, the epiphytic species find a home in the leaf litter on the branches and trunks of trees and shrubs, in the same way as many orchid species; epiphytes are in no way parasitic on their host plants. Southern India has many such plants, all with colorful flowers. The remainder of Indian species fall into the last, broad group that encompasses a wide range of annual and perennial species, including a few almost shrubby plants.

Some Indian species have been grown in botanical gardens for many years, but few have yet come into general horticulture. One exception is *Impatiens balsamina*, which has been grown in Western gardens for centuries. This species is one of the most widespread species across Asia; it grows throughout India, and is the only *Impatiens* species found in both the north and south of the country. *Impatiens balsamina* is one of the few species that has fairly long seed viability, which probably accounts for its very wide natural distribution. In the wild this annual species grows to about 1 m in height, with single flowers in various colors from purple and red to white. *Impatiens balsamina* has been hybridized extensively, with the most popular garden form being the dwarf, double camellia-flowered hybrids, which are sold by most seed merchants.

Impatiens chinensis is another Indian species that is very widespread, commonly found growing in subtropical Asian countries, such as China, Thailand, and Vietnam. This species is shorter than *I. balsamina*, growing to only about 50 cm tall. *Impatiens chinensis* prefers marshy ground and usually forms large colonies. The flower color range is from deep pink to almost white, often with purple markings. From a horticultural perspective, its only drawback is that it tends to flower late in the season.

One of the most eye-catching plants is *Impatiens grandis*, which has some of the largest flowers in the genus, reaching 5–7 cm in diameter. The flowers are usually white, but sometimes light pink with a varying degree of deep red central markings. The plant grows to 2 m in height and has fairly large leaves. Although spectacular when in full flower, *I. grandis* is another late flowerer, but it is an ideal candidate for the heated greenhouse or conservatory. A close relative is *I. campanulata*, which is superficially like *I. grandis* but with smaller, slightly bell-shaped flowers. *Impatiens campanulata* also produces white flowers with purple and red central markings, but differs by flowering throughout the season.

Of the subshrubby species, *Impatiens leschenaultia* and *I. latifolia* are both free-flowering, providing a fine show throughout the late spring and summer. *Impatiens leschenaultia* has creamy white flowers with a yellow spur, whereas *I. latifolia* produces pinkish lilac flowers. Both species can grow to more than 1 m in height, tending to get a little woody near the base. When grown in large pots and wintered in a frost-free greenhouse, these species will produce flowers for most of the year. Another subshrubby species is *I. cuspidata*, which has white to pale pink flowers. This species also grows to about 1 m tall, with its stems and branches completely covered with an extraordinary white powdery farina, making it stand out, especially in low light conditions.

Impatiens maculata is a tall plant found growing near rivers and streams. As its name implies, its stems and branches are marked with dark, almost black spots. This species produces large pink flowers that are delightfully pleated or crinkled like a concertina.

Southern India has many low-growing species with a tendency to creep or trail, some of which would be ideal for patio planting. *Impatiens cordata* is a very attractive perennial trailing plant with small, shiny leaves and large, light purple flowers, with two darker purple blotches at the center. *Impatiens repens* is another good trailing plant, with succulent reddish stems and large, pouched, yellow flowers that are much larger than its leaves. *Impatiens repens* is not native to India, however, although it has become naturalized in many parts of the country. Its home is Sri Lanka, where until fairly recently it was thought to have gone extinct, but fortunately it has now been rediscovered.

Impatiens repens has been grown in many botanical gardens for some time, making a fine indoor hanging basket plant.

Impatiens phoenicea is certainly a potential candidate for Western gardens. The plant is slightly shrubby but not too large. This species produces masses of bright scarlet flowers with bright yellow centers; the flowers are cup-shaped, with incurving spurs. Another lovely red-flowered species is *I. verticillata*, which has very showy orange-red, flat flowers that stand out against its shiny, dark green leaves. As its name suggests, the leaves are arranged in whorls or verticils. *Impatiens verticillata* particularly enjoys a position near rivers or streams and can often be found growing in flowing water, especially during periods of high rainfall.

Of the scapigerous group, *Impatiens scapiflora* is by far the most common and is found in many parts of southern India. This species is also the most variable in size, ranging from 10 to 30 cm in height. Its leaves can grow to 20 cm in diameter, and the flowers, which are borne on long scapes, are a delicate shade of light pink. *Impatiens scapiflora* is often confused with *I. acaulis*, which is also found in many of the same locations in southern India. However, *I. acaulis* is also found in Sri Lanka and is the only one of this group that is found there. The two species are easily distinguished by their flowers: in *I. scapiflora* the lower petals are deeply bilobed, whereas in *I. acaulis* they are single lobed. *Impatiens levingei* is a small, stemless plant with thick, fleshy, heart-shaped leaves. Its pale purple, star-shaped flowers are held on scapes reaching 15–20 cm high, and they open in succession over a few weeks. This is another species that grows near running water in its native habitat.

The Nilgiri Hills in Tamil Nadu are home to many endemic species, and recently a few were rediscovered after not being seen in the wild for more than 80 years. *Impatiens nilgirica* is a very small plant with beautiful, heavily hooded, purple-red pouched flowers. *Impatiens laticornis* is similar in habit but produces pale lilac flowers, which bear characteristic tufts of purple hairs at the center. Both of these plants are still quite rare and only found in a few isolated places in the Nilgiri Hills. Another is the very small and unusual *I. orchioides*, often found growing epiphytically on moss-covered branches or fallen trees, like many of the epiphytic orchids of the region. *Impatiens orchioides* bears small, brick red, star-shaped flowers on short scapes.

Within the epiphytic group we can find a few remarkable species, both in color and habit. These species are not plentiful, indeed some are very rare, but *Impatiens parasitica* is probably the most common. This is a very attractive plant, and its red and yellowish green flowers can often be seen almost completely covering the branches of some trees, providing quite a spectacular display. Many color variations are to be found within this species, ranging from magenta to orange to green. The epiphyte *I. auriculata* is unusual in that it has very large lateral sepals that nearly cover the entire flower, like the wings of a small bird. Perhaps the rarest species within this group is the recently described *I. violacea*, a beautiful plant with violet-blue and yellow flowers. Reports suggest that fewer than 50 plants remain in the wild, mainly due to the deforestation of many of its habitats. Attempts have been made to re-establish *I. violacea*, but so far without much success.

Impatiens jerdoniae is another epiphytic species with red and yellow flowers, which also shows a good deal of color variation. In comparison to the size of the plant, the deeply pouched flowers are large, sometimes as long as 5 cm. The flowers are normally laterally compressed but can occasionally be found in inflated forms. *Impatiens jerdoniae* plants have extraordinarily shaped, moniliform stems. This growth form is caused by the growing period being so short that the very succulent stems lose all their leaves during the dry periods, regrowing again to their normal size at the commencement of the next wet period. The result is a plant made up of a string of short, thick, sausage-shaped stems, with the length of each segment being determined by the length of the monsoon period. When grown under cultivation, however, the stems grow much like those of other impatiens.

The Species

Impatiens acaulis Arnott

Stemless, succulent species growing to 15–20 cm high from small underground tubers. Leaves arising directly from these, on petioles, 6–10 cm long, ovate to suborbicular, margins serrated, teeth forward pointing. Flowers white to rose, 3–4.5 cm across, on scapes 10–25 cm long, bearing six to 10 blooms; lateral sepals small, linear-ovate, reddish dark green, lower sepal whitish, boat-shaped, abruptly narrowing into a long, thin spur; dorsal petal small, hooded; lateral united petals 3 cm, rose colored, upper petals oblong, curving upward, lower petals longer, straight, downward pointing. Seed capsule fusiform, 1 cm long. *Impatiens acaulis* is found on wet rocks and damp riverbanks in the western Ghats at Karnatica, Tamil Nadu, and Kerala as well as in Sri Lanka.

Impatiens
auriculata

Impatiens auriculata Wight

An epiphytic, perennial species growing to 25–30 cm tall, stems very fleshy and swollen. Leaves alternate, broadly ovate-lanceolate, obscurely crenate, with glandular hairs at the base, 2–17 cm long by 1–6 cm wide, petioles 1–4 cm long. Flowers red and yellow, single or in pairs in leaf axils; lateral sepals very large and pendulous, obliquely ovate, pointed, scarlet, almost completely covering the lower sepal, lower sepal deeply saccate, purplish green, laterally compressed with short hooked spur; dorsal petal small, dark green, hooded, lateral petals almost hidden by lower sepal, purple. Seed capsule fusiform, 8 mm long. *Impatiens auriculata* is found in the southwestern Ghats in southern Kerala and Tamil Nadu.

Impatiens balsamina Linnaeus

An erect, annual species, growing to 80 cm tall, simple or sparsely branched. Leaves arranged alternately, smooth, lanceolate-elliptical, margins serrate, 5–15 cm long by 2–3 cm wide, petioles 3–10 cm long. Flowers solitary or sometimes in pairs, purple or white, occasionally red, on short pedicels; lateral sepals ovate, lower sepal shortly pouched, narrowing to an incurving spur, 2–3 cm long; dorsal petal orbicular, 1.2 cm in diameter, with shallow dorsal crest; lateral united petals 2–2.5 cm long, lower larger than upper, notched. Seed capsule pendent, ellipsoid, heavily tomentose. *Impatiens balsamina* is one of the most widespread species in Asia, growing throughout India, China, Thailand, and Vietnam.

Impatiens campanulata Wight

Erect, robust, sparsely branched perennial species, growing to 1.5 m tall. Leaves arranged alternately, smooth, broadly ovate, serrate, 7–15 cm long by 3–6 cm wide, petioles 2.5–5 cm long. Flowers creamy white, speckled with red and purple, 2.5 cm, in umbels of two or three; lateral sepals broadly ovate, large, lower sepal boat-shaped with short spur; dorsal petal orbicular, with dorsal keel, lateral petals 1.5–2 cm long, upper pair smaller than lower pair. Seed capsule spindle-shaped, 1.5–2 cm long. *Impatiens campanulata* is found in the western Ghats, in Nilgiri, Anamalai, and Pulney Hills.

Impatiens campanulata

Impatiens chinensis Linnaeus

Erect, slender, succulent herb growing to 30–40 cm high. Leaves opposite, sessile, linear to lanceolate, serrate, prominent teeth, dark green, 3–7 cm long by 0.5–1 cm wide. Flowers large, white to dark pink; lateral sepals linear, pointed, 7 mm long, lower sepal funnel-shaped, abruptly constricted into a curved spur, 2 cm long; dorsal petal small hooded, suborbital, lateral petals 1.5–2.5 cm long, upper pair ovate-triangular, lower pair much larger, broadly elliptical, slightly emarginated. Seed capsule spindle-shaped, 1.5 cm long. *Impatiens chinensis* is a very widespread species found in India, China, Tibet, Malaysia, and Vietnam.

Impatiens coelotropis C. Fischer

Lax subshrub, erect to prostrate, growing to about 1 m in height, succulent, becoming woody, stems sparsely branched, rooting at the nodes. Leaves arranged alternately, ovate to lanceolate, margins serrate, 5–13 cm long by 2.5–6 cm wide, petioles 1.5–7 cm long, red with stipitate glands. Flowers 2.7 cm long, red and green, in axillary racemes of three or four; lateral sepals thick, ovate-lanceolate, red, lower sepal deeply pouched, laterally com-

Impatiens coelotropis

Impatiens cordata

pressed, 1.8 cm long, with upward pointed thick spur, bright glossy green, shading to scarlet at the mouth; dorsal petal suborbicular, hooded, pointed at front, 1.5 cm long, with red dorsal keel, lateral petals 1.5 cm long, top overlapping bottom. Seed capsule fusiform, 1.5 cm long, glossy. *Impatiens coelotropis* is found in the western Ghats, on the slopes of the Anaimudi Hills in Kerala.

Impatiens cordata Wight

Decumbent to slightly erect perennial herb, growing to 15–30 cm high, stems mainly prostrate, rooting at the nodes. Leaves alternate, ovate-cordate, with glossy surface, obscurely crenate, 4–7 cm long by 3–4.5 cm wide, petioled. Flowers single or in pairs, lilac with two purple marks at center or white with red centers; lateral sepals large, ovate, lower funnel-shaped, narrowing into slender, incurved spur; dorsal petal orbicular, small; lateral united petals 2.5 cm, upper very small, incurved, lower petals much larger and spreading wider. Seed capsule spindle-shaped, slightly beaked, 1 cm long. *Impatiens cordata* is found in the western Ghats at Tamil Nadu and Kerala.

Impatiens cuspidata Wight & Arnott

A subshrub growing to 50–100 cm high, stems and branches glaucous, sometimes completely covered with a white farina. Leaves opposite, alternate or whorled, elliptical-lanceolate, margins serrate, 5–10 cm long by 2–4.5 cm wide, glandular at lower margins, petiole 1.5–5 cm long. Flowers palest pink to white, 2.5–3 cm across, solitary or in pairs, in leaf axils; lateral sepals minute, lower sepal funnel-shaped, gradually narrowing into a thin spur, 1.5–2 cm long; dorsal petal 1.5–2 cm wide, deeply emarginate; lateral united petals 2 cm, upper larger than lower, elliptical, spreading. Seed capsule fusiform, 2.2 cm long. *Impatiens cuspidata* is found in the western Ghats at Karnatica, Tamil Nadu, and Kerala, as well as in Sri Lanka.

Impatiens disotis Hooker f.

Erect perennial herb growing to about 1 m in height, sparsely branched. Leaves alternate, broadly elliptical, serrate margins, 7–15 cm long by 4–6 cm wide, membranous, petioled. Flowers creamy white with dark purple in the throat, 2.5–3 cm; lateral sepals ovate, pointed, lower sepal funnel-shaped with short spur; dorsal petal orbicular, emarginated at top; lateral united petals 2.5 cm long, upper pair small, ovate, lower much larger, wider. Seed capsule fusiform, 2 cm long. *Impatiens disotis* is found in the western Ghats, at Travancore, Tinnavelli Hills, Tamil Nadu, and Kerala.

Impatiens flaccida Arnott

Erect to decumbent herb, growing to 50 cm high, stems slender, sparsely branched in lower half, green flushed with pink, rooting at lower nodes. Leaves alternate, ovate-lanceolate, margins crenate, 3–8 cm long by 2–3.5 cm wide, sparsely pubescent, petioled, with stipitate glands, flowers light purple, with darker eye, 3–4 cm across, solitary or in fascicles of two or three; lateral sepals ovate, lower sepal funnel-shaped narrowing into a slender, filiform, slightly incurving spur; dorsal petal obcordate, deeply emarginated, dorsally keeled, terminating in an acute point; lateral united petals 2.5 cm long, upper and lower petals equal in size, both obovate, with slight emargination. Seed capsule fusiform, 1.5 cm long. *Impatiens flaccida* is found in the western Ghats at Karnataka, Tamil Nadu, and Kerala, as well as in Sri Lanka.

Impatiens fruticosa Leschen ex DC

Erect, shrubby, perennial species, growing to over 2 m in height, branched, slightly glaucous. Leaves arranged alternately, ovate to ovate-elliptical, margins crenate, glandular near base, 7–13 cm long by 3.5–5 cm wide, pubescent, petioles 2–7 cm long. Flowers white with pink at the center, 3.5–4 cm wide, single or in pairs; lateral sepals ovate, pointed, 1.6 cm long by 0.6 cm wide, tomentose, lower sepal funnel-shaped, gradually narrowing into a curved spur, 2.5 cm long; dorsa petal orbicular, 2 cm, emarginate at top; lateral petals 2.5 cm, upper ovate, lower larger, both lateral petals reflexing. Seed capsule fusiform, 2 cm. *Impatiens fruticosa* is found in the western Ghats at Tamil Nadu and Kerala.

Impatiens gardneriana Wight

An annual species, growing to 30–60 cm tall, upright or creeping at the base, simple or branched. Leaves opposite or whorled, ovate-oblong, leaf margins serrate, 3–12 cm long by 1–4 cm wide, sparsely pubescent, petioled. Flowers deep pink to purple, 2.5 cm across, in axils, single or in pairs; lateral sepals ovate, lower sepal funnel-shaped, upward curved spur, 1.5–1.8 cm long; dorsal petal suborbicular, dorsally keeled; lateral united petals 2 cm long, upper obovate, lower petals larger. Seed capsule spindle-shaped, 1.5 cm long. *Impa-*

tiens gardneriana is found in the evergreen forests of the western Ghats at Tamil Nadu and Kerala.

Impatiens grandis Heyne

Shrubby, erect, perennial herb, growing to over 2 m high, leaves confined mainly to the top portion of the stem, glabrous, alternate, serrate, 8–20 cm long by 3–8 cm wide, with two glands at base, petioles 2–10 cm long. Flowers large, 4–6 cm wide, white to pale rose, with central dark red markings, flat-faced, in umbels of four to six in upper leaf axils; lateral sepals ovate, lower sepal funnel-shaped, narrowing into stout, straight spur, 4 cm long; dorsal petal orbicular, notched at top; lateral united petals 2–3 cm long, upper pair ovate, lower longer and wider. Seed capsule ellipsoid. *Impatiens grandis* is found growing in the western Ghats at Tamil Nadu and in Sri Lanka.

Impatiens grandis Christopher Grey-Wilson

Impatiens henslowiana Arnott

An upright, shrubby, perennial plant, growing to 1–1.5 m high, little branched, succulent when young, discarding lower leaves with age. Leaves arranged alternately, elliptical-lanceolate, margins serrate, 4–14 cm long by 2–5 cm wide, almost glabrous to pilose, petioled. Flowers white, 4–5 cm across, solitary or

Impatiens henslowiana

in small fascicles; lateral sepals ovate, lower sepal funnel-shaped, narrowing into slender, incurving spur, 4.5–6 cm long; dorsal petal almost orbicular, emarginated at top, with erect dorsal keel; lateral united petals 2.5–3 cm long, upper pair obovate, notched, lower pair longer, also notched. Seed capsule fusiform, 2–2.5 cm long. *Impatiens henslowiana* is found in the western Ghats at Tamil Nadu and Kerala, as well as in Sri Lanka.

Impatiens jerdoniae Wight

Succulent epiphytic herb, growing to 15–30 cm tall, stems very thick, green or purplish, swollen at internodes. Leaves few, alternate, elliptical, pointed, margins serrate, 5–8 cm long, deep green with glandular cilia near the base, petioles stout, long. Flowers scarlet and yellow, solitary or in pairs, 3.5–5 cm long, on long peduncles 2.5–8 cm long; lateral sepals lanceolate, pointed, dark green, lower sepal 3–4.5 cm long, deeply saccate, latterly compressed, wrinkled, with upward pointed spur; dorsal petal yellow, orbicular, hooded, with narrow dorsal keel; lateral united petals small, concealed by the mouth of lower sepal. Seed capsule fusiform, 6–8 mm long. *Impatiens jerdoniae* is found growing on the trunks of trees or on rocks in the western Ghats at Karnatica (Brahmagiri), Tamil Nadu (Nilgiri, Anamalai, and Pulney Hills), and Kerala. This is a beautiful and colorful species that has many varieties, both in color and form.

Impatiens
jerdoniae

Impatiens johnii Barnes

Erect shrub, growing to about 1 m high, branches from base, with swollen nodes. Leaves opposite, alternate, or whorled, ovate-elliptical, margins crenate-serrate, 5–13 cm long by 5 cm wide, hairy on top surface, petioles 8 cm long. Flowers pink, solitary, in leaf axils, 4 cm long; lateral sepals ovate, 1.3 cm long, ciliate along margins, lower sepal funnel-shaped, narrowing into slender, curved spur, 4 cm long, shading to crimson at lower end; dorsal petal small, hooded, dorsally keeled; lateral united petals 3 cm long, upper pair narrowly elliptical, spreading, lower pair slightly longer, also elliptical. Seed capsule spindle-shaped, beaked, 2.8 cm long. *Impatiens johnii* can be found along streambeds in the western Ghats at Kerala.

Impatiens latifolia Linnaeus

Erect, branched subshrub, growing to 1–1.5 m tall, stems and branches pinkish red. Leaves alternate, ovate, 5–12 cm long by 2–2.5 cm wide, margins crenate-serrate, thinly textured, petioled. Flowers solitary or sometimes in pairs, 2–2.5 cm long, light purple to pink; lateral sepals small to minute, ovate, lower sepal funnel-shaped, narrowing into a straight, short spur, 1.2–2 cm long; dorsal petal orbicular, 1 cm across, lateral petals 2 cm long, upper shorter than the lower. Seed capsule fusiform, 1–2 cm long. *Impatiens latifolia* is found in the southwestern Ghats, from Tamil Nadu to Karnatica.

Impatiens leptopoda Arnott

Perennial species, growing to 70 cm or more, much branched, erect, but sometimes decumbent and then rooting at the lower nodes, green or reddish. Leaves arranged alternately, dark green, lanceolate-elliptical, 2–10 cm long by 1–3 cm wide, with darkish glands near the base, petioled. Flowers pink to white, with dark magenta spot at base, solitary or in fascicles of two or three; lateral sepals linear-lanceolate, pointed, lower sepal shallowly boat-shaped, constricting into a curved, filiform spur, 2.5 cm long; dorsal petal obcordate, 1 cm across, lateral petals 7–10 mm long, upper petals almost covering the much smaller lower petals. Seed capsule fusiform, 1.3 cm long. *Impatiens leptopoda* is only found in Sri Lanka.

Impatiens leschenaultii Wallich

Leafy shrub, growing to 1.5 m or more in height. Leaves opposite, alternate, or whorled, glabrous, leaf margins crenate, petioles 5 cm long. Flowers white, with yellow spurs, solitary or in pairs; lateral sepals ovate-lanceolate, 3 mm

Impatiens leschenaultii

long, lower sepal funnel-shaped, narrowing into thin, incurved spur; dorsal petal suborbicular, 1.5 cm with dorsal crest; lateral united petals 2 cm long, upper oblong, smaller than lower. Seed capsule fusiform, 1.8 cm long. *Impatiens leschenaultii* is found in the western Ghats at Tamil Nadu and Kerala.

Impatiens levingei Gamble

Stemless species growing from underground tubers. Leaves fleshy, orbicular, 3–6 cm wide, petioles 8–10 cm long, margins obscurely crenate. Flowers pale purple, in racemes of six to 10 on scapes 12–25 cm tall; lateral sepals tiny, ovate, lower sepal boat-shaped with curved tubular spur, 1 cm long; dorsal petal small, hooded, lateral petals 1 cm long, upper small, oblong, lower bilobed. Seed capsule fusiform, 5 mm long. *Impatiens levingei* is usually found growing on wet rocks and streams in Tamil Nadu and Kerala.

*Impatiens
levingei*

Impatiens macrophylla

Impatiens macrophylla Gardner ex Hooker

Robust, shrubby perennial species growing to over 2 m tall, stems erect, branched near the base, succulent, reddish, becoming woody with age. Leaves arranged alternately, slightly pubescent when young, 11–22 cm long by 6–8 cm wide, ovate to almost elliptical, margins serrate, fringed at base with long, soft bristles. Flowers small for the size of plant, deep tawny orange; lateral sepals small, ovate, lower sepal cupped, constricted into a short, very recurved, bifid, swollen spur; dorsal petal red, hooded, ovate, terminating with a claw-shaped point; lateral united petals small, upper petals oblong, lower petals longer, ovate. Seed capsule fusiform, 1.5 cm long. *Impatiens macrophylla* is only found in Sri Lanka.

Impatiens maculata Wight

Tall, shrubby herb, growing to 2 m in height, slender erect stems, branches angled or ribbed, greenish pink, with dark spots or blotches. Leaves alternate, ovate-lanceolate, margins serrate, 7.5–12 cm long by 3–5 cm wide, hairy on upper and lower surfaces, petioles 2.5–3 cm long, glanduliferous, with two or more long, stipitate glands. Flowers light pink or white, 2.5–3 cm, in many-flowered racemes; lateral sepals ovate, pointed, lower sepal with 3-cm slender, upward, incurving spur; dorsal petal small, hooded; lateral united petals 3 cm, upper minute and concealed, lower petals suborbicular, very large, crinkled or pleated. Seed capsule fusiform, five-angled, beaked, 1 cm long. *Impatiens maculata* is found near the banks of montane rivers or streams in Tamil Nadu and Kerala.

Impatiens munronii Wight

Subshrub growing to 60 cm tall, hairy, branched, woody at base. Leaves alternate, elliptical-ovate, serrulate, glandular at margins, 3–8 cm long by 1.5–3 cm wide, membranous, hairy on upper and lower surfaces, petioles 1.5–5 cm long. Flowers red, 1.5–2.5 cm, in leaf axils, solitary; lateral sepals ovate-lanceolate, green, hairy, lower sepal funnel-shaped, narrowing to incurved, green, hairy spur, 1.5 cm long; dorsal petal heavily hooded, orbicular, with dorsal keel; lateral united petals 1.5 cm, upper short, oblong, lower larger. Seed capsule spindle-shaped, hairy, 1 cm long. *Impatiens munronii* is quite variable in color and found in the Tamil Nadu area.

Impatiens neo-barnsii C. Fischer

Rather delicate, stemless epiphytic plant, pendulous, growing to 5–7 cm tall, arising from small bulbous tubers. Leaves one or two, ovate or elliptical-ovate, pointed at apex, margins remotely denticulate, 2–8 cm long by 1.5–3.5 wide, sparsely hairy or glabrous above. Flowers cream to almost white, delicate, 2–2.5 cm on few-flowered scapes, 4–6 cm long; lateral sepals two, ovate, 5 mm long, lower sepal almost orbicular, 1 cm long, with tiny, incurving spur; dorsal petal suborbicular, hooded; lateral united petals 2–2.5 cm long, upper petals oblong, lower petals oblong-lanceolate, slightly emarginate. Seed capsule fusiform, 8 mm long. *Impatiens neo-barnsii* is found on moss-covered tree trunks in wet shoal forests in the Nilgiri Hills.

Impatiens nilgirica C. Fischer

Erect, stemless plants, growing from small bulbous underground tubers. Leaves one or two, radical, suborbicular, with crenate margins, 2.5–4 cm wide, fleshy, petioles 3–9 cm long, purplish. Flowers purple and crimson, on 20-cm scapes carrying four to 10 flowers; lateral sepals two, small, ovate, green, lower sepal 1 cm, with short incurved spur; dorsal petal hooded, orbicular, lateral petals 2 cm long, upper small, oblong, forward pointing, lower petals larger, bilobed, spreading, lower lobe downward pointed. Seed capsule fusiform, 1.2 cm long. *Impatiens nilgirica* is a very rare species only found in the Nilgiri Hills of the western Ghats, in the Kundah Range of Tamil Nadu.

Impatiens oppositifolia Linnaeus

Erect annual species, growing to 60 cm tall, with slender branches. Leaves opposite, 2.5–7 cm long, linear-oblong, serrated edges, sparsely hairy. Flowers pale pink to white, 1.2 cm across, single or in small fascicles; lateral sepals linear-lanceolate, pointed, lower sepal slightly saccate, with short, stout, incurved spur; dorsal petal orbicular, hooded; lateral united petals 1 cm, upper pair small, falcate, lower larger, obovate, clawed. Seed capsule fusiform, 1–1.2 long. *Impatiens oppositifolia* is often found in grasslands and open pastures in the western Ghats at Karnatica, Tamil Nadu, and Kerala, as well as in Sri Lanka.

Impatiens orchioides Beddome

Epiphytic, stemless herb with tuberous rootstock. Leaves radical, ovate, orbicular, deeply cordate at base, margins bristly crenate, 1–5 cm long by 1–6 cm wide, surface hairy, petioles 2–16 cm long. Flowers brick red and pale brown, 8 mm across; lateral sepals small, ovate, lower sepal ovate, spurless; dorsal petal ovate, lateral petals 7 mm, upper pointed, lower bilobed, both lobes pointed. Seed capsule fusiform. *Impatiens orchioides* is another very rare species, endemic to the Nilgiri Hills of Tamil Nadu.

*Impatiens
parasitica*

Impatiens parasitica Beddome

Epiphytic, succulent herbs growing to 15–35 cm high. Stems moniliform, green to purplish, with swollen internodes. Leaves crowded at the ends of stems, ovate-elliptical, pointed, margins serrate, with glandular cilia at base, 3–7 cm long by 2–3 cm wide, petioles 2–6 cm long. Flowers red and greenish yellow, 2–2.5 cm long; lateral sepals linear, dark green, pointed, 0.5 mm long, lower sepal deeply saccate, red, narrowing to small upturned spur, held in vertical position; dorsal petal small, hooded, greenish yellow and turning yellow with age, dorsally keeled, lateral petals very small, partially concealed by lower sepal. Seed capsule fusiform, 5–7 mm long. *Impatiens parasitica* is found growing on the trunks and branches of trees and shrubs in Tamil Nadu and Kerala (Anamalai Hills). Several nurseries in Europe and the United States have been offering this species for some time, as it makes a fine indoor pot plant, flowering for most of the year. Many color variations are known.

Impatiens phoenicea Beddome

Almost shrubby, erect plant, 50–80 cm tall, branched, spreading. Leaves arranged alternately, smooth, ovate-lanceolate, leaf margins serrate-crenate, 5–15 cm long by 2.5–3.5 cm wide, dark green. Flowers bright scarlet red, with yellow at the centers, 2.5 cm long; lateral sepals ovate, lower sepal funnel-shaped, narrowing into an incurving spur, 2.5 cm long; dorsal petal scarlet, broad, ovate; lateral united petals scarlet with some yellow at the center, upper petals heart-shaped, lower oblong. Seed capsules 2 cm long, spindle-shaped. *Impatiens phoenicea* grows in the Pulney Hills of Tamil Nadu and in Kerala.

Impatiens platyadena C. Fischer

Subshrub growing to about 1 m in height, angled stems. Leaves arranged alternately, elliptical-lanceolate, 8–17 cm long by 3.5–7 cm wide, crenate-serrate, with four to eight white marginal glands. Flowers scarlet red and creamy white, 1.5–2.5 cm long, in slender axillary racemes; lateral sepals suborbicular, 0.6 mm wide, cream colored, lower sepal funnel-shaped, narrowing into incurved spur, 1.5–2 cm long; dorsal petal ovate, 8 mm long, hooded; lateral united petals 1.5–2 cm long, upper petals ovate-triangular, lower much longer and wider, bright scarlet. Seed capsule spindle-shaped, 1.5 cm long. *Impatiens platyadena* is a beautiful species found in high-elevation grasslands in the western Ghats at Kerala.

Impatiens raziana Baskar & Razi

Prostrate to decumbent annual herb, rooting at the nodes, branches opposite, rising from lower nodes, 15–18 cm long, stems quadrangular. Leaves opposite, ovate, 0.5 cm by 1 cm, petiolate. Flowers solitary, scarlet; lateral sepals linear, lower sepal minute, tinged yellow, tiny spur; dorsal petal orbicular, lateral petals ovate, fin-shaped, lower larger, orbicular. Seed capsule 0.5 cm long. *Impatiens raziana* is only found in Karnatica.

Impatiens repens Moon

A procumbent or trailing, succulent, perennial plant with pinkish red stems, growing to 30–50 cm long, much branched, rooting at the nodes. Leaves arranged alternately, small, heart-shaped, dark green, smooth, margins serrate. Flowers large, yellow, single; lateral sepals small, ovate, greenish, lower sepal saccate, narrowing to a short thin spur, swollen at the tip; dorsal petal large, hooded; lateral united petals 2 cm long, upper pair ovate, lower longer and wider. Seed capsule 1 cm long, fusiform, pilose. *Impatiens repens* is endemic to Sri Lanka and has been grown in numerous botanical gardens for many years. It makes an ideal subject for indoor hanging baskets and has been offered by a few nurseries from time to time.

Impatiens scabriuscula Heyne ex Roxburgh

Erect herb growing to 10–20 cm in height, stems branching at base, hairy. Leaves alternate, elliptical-lanceolate, margins serrate, 1.6–6 cm long by 1 cm wide, sparsely hairy above, petiole 3 mm long. Flowers very small, white to pale pink; lateral sepals minute, lower sepal spurless; dorsal petal orbicular, hooded, lateral petals 1 cm long, upper petals small, lower petals oblong-ovate. Seed capsule hairy, 0.8 cm long. *Impatiens scabriuscula* is found in the western Ghats at Maharashtra, Karnataka, Tamil Nadu, and Kerala.

Impatiens scapiflora Heyne

Stemless herb with tuberous rootstock, growing to 15–45 cm tall. Leaves radical, variable, orbicular, ovate, or reniform, crenate or serrate along leaf margins, 5–20 cm long by 3–15 cm wide, fleshy and hairy on upper surface, sometimes glabrous, pale green below, petioles up to 20 cm long. Flowers pink, 2.5–3 cm across, on 7- to 30-cm scapes, with many-flowered racemes; lateral sepals very small, linear-lanceolate, lower sepal funnel-shaped, abruptly

*Impatiens
repens*

*Impatiens
scapiflora*

constricting into a long thin spur, 2.5–3.5 cm long; dorsal petal orbicular, 5 mm, hooded, lateral petals 2.5–3 cm, upper pair oblanceolate, falcate, lower pair linear-oblong, bilobed. Seed capsule fusiform, 1.2 cm long. *Impatiens scapiflora* is found in many places in the western Ghats, including Karnatica, Tamil Nadu, and Kerala, mainly on wet or moist ground or rocks in evergreen forests.

Impatiens sholayarensis M. Kumar & Sequiera

Epiphytic species with fleshy, succulent stems, growing to 5 cm long, moniliform. Leaves crowded near the apex of the stem, ovate or elliptical-lanceolate 2.5–8 cm long by 1.5–3.5 cm wide, with two prominent glands near base, margins crenulated, petioles 2.5–8 cm long. Flowers greenish yellow and crimson red, in pairs; lateral sepals small, linear, pointed, lower sepal saccate, laterally compressed, 1–3.5 cm long, yellow shading below to crimson, prominently hooked at the mouth, abruptly narrowed into a very curved spur, tipped with white; dorsal petal hooded, with shallow dorsal keel; lateral united petals very small, almost hidden inside the mouth of the lower sepal. Seed capsule fusiform, 1 cm long. *Impatiens sholayarensis* is a very rare species, only known to grow in the western Ghats at Kerala and Sholayar.

Impatiens tomentosa Heyne

Erect herbs growing to 30–40 cm in height, stems reddish, hairy above. Leaves opposite, elliptical to ovate-oblong, serrulate with reddish tips, 1.5–3 cm long by 0.6–1.2 wide, slightly hairy, petioles 3 mm long. Flowers small, 1 cm across, in leaf axils, solitary, pinkish shading to yellow; lateral sepals linear-lanceolate, ciliate, lower sepal deeply saccate, hairy on outside, with short, hooked spur; dorsal petal orbicular with short dorsal keel, lateral petals small, upper petals oblong, lower petals longer, orbicular. Seed capsule spindle-shaped, 1.2 cm long. *Impatiens tomentosa* is found in boggy areas or swamps in the western Ghats at Karnatica and Kerala.

Impatiens umbellata Heyne

Annual herbs growing to 10–20 cm high, simple, rarely branched. Leaves ovate-elliptical, sometimes orbicular, margins broadly crenate, 2.5–5 cm long by 2.5 cm wide, often dark brown or purplish beneath. Flowers light purple or pink, in umbels of one to six; lateral sepals broadly ovate, lower sepal boat-shaped, narrowing into a long, slender, incurving spur, 2.5 cm long; dorsal petal orbicular; lateral united petals almost equal in size. Seed capsule fusiform, 1 cm long. *Impatiens umbellata* is found in Tamil Nadu and Kerala.

Impatiens verticillata Wight

Herb or subshrub, growing to 60 cm in height, branched in lower half, swollen at nodes. Leaves opposite or in whorls of three to six, dark green, elliptical to elliptical-lanceolate, crenate-serrate, 6–12 cm long by 1.2–2.2 cm wide, petioled. Flowers scarlet red, 3–3.5 cm across, in umbels

Impatiens verticillata

of three to six, in upper leaf axils; lateral sepals linear-lanceolate, 1 cm long, lower sepal funnel-shaped, narrowing into slender curved spur; dorsal petal hooded, orbicular, slightly emarginate at top 0.5–1 cm; lateral united petals 2.5 cm long, upper petals oblong, curving upward, lower petals longer and wider. Seed capsule fusiform, 1.2 cm long. *Impatiens verticillata* is usually found in gravely stream- or riverbeds in the western Ghats at Tamil Nadu and Kerala. This species has a great potential for western gardens.

Impatiens violacea

Impatiens violacea M. Kumar & Sequiera

Epiphytic, succulent, perennial species, growing to 10–15 cm long, thick stemmed, with leaves crowded near the top of stem. Leaves ovate to ovate-lanceolate, margins crenulated-serrate, 2–6 cm long by 1.5–4 cm wide, pointed, purplish green, petioles 3–5 cm long, channeled, with two stipitate glands near base. Flowers purplish blue and yellow, in short racemes of one to three; lateral sepals linear-lanceolate, dark green, lower sepal deeply saccate, violet blue, 2 cm long, laterally compressed,

*Impatiens
violacea*

with side creases and short hooked spur; dorsal petal yellow with some green, hooded, lateral petals small, concealed by lower sepal. Seed capsule fusiform, 1 cm long. *Impatiens violacea* is a very rare species only known to grow in the Pettimudi area of Munnar, Kerala.

Impatiens viscida Wight

Slender herb, growing to 1 m in height, branching, rooting at lower nodes, stem angular. Leaves alternate, elliptical-lanceolate, margins serrate, 5–8 cm long by 1.5–3 cm wide, veins on both surfaces covered with stiff hairs. Flowers deep pink to light purple, 2.5–3 cm wide, in short racemes; lateral sepals suborbicular, small, lower sepal boat-shaped, narrowing into long spur; dorsal petal small, hooded, lateral petals 2.5–3 cm, upper petals small, ovate, lower petals very much larger, orbicular. Seed capsule fusiform, beaked, 1.5 cm long. *Impatiens viscida* is found mainly in the Pulney Hills of Tamil Nadu.

Impatiens wightiana Beddome

Erect, shrubby, perennial herb growing to 40 cm high, branched, rooting at lower nodes. Leaves alternate, ovate to ovate-lanceolate, serrate, 5–18 cm long by 2–4.5 wide, smooth, petioles 3–8 cm long, with many glands. Flowers in 11-cm racemes, in leaf axils, white mottled with pink, 1–1.5 cm across; lat-

Impatiens wightiana

eral sepals small, lower sepal funnel-shaped, with short, hooked spur; dorsal petal small, ovate, hooded; upper lateral petals small, triangular, lower petals much longer and wider, 2.5 cm long, almost crescent-shaped. Seed capsule bursiform, 1 cm long. *Impatiens wightiana* is a rare species, confined to the Anamalai Hills in Kerala.

11

Impatiens of Southeast Asia

Southeast Asia provides us with some beautiful and bizarre impatiens, none more so than *Impatiens mirabilis*. Found in southern Thailand and some of the islands off the coast of Malaya, it is surely the most extraordinary of all *Impatiens* species. Indeed, the habit is so different that it hardly seems possible that it could be a member of the genus at all. The plant can best be described as a slow-growing, cruciform succulent, eventually forming a small tree up to 3 m high, with a trunk 50 cm in diameter or more and topped with a crown of very large leaves. Although small in comparison to the plant's size, the flowers are quite large and form racemes of four or five blooms. The usual flower color is golden yellow, but white, pink, and apricot color variations can be found.

The islands of Langkawi are almost entirely composed of limestone rock, as is the southern coast of Thailand. *Impatiens mirabilis* can be found among the huge limestone boulders that litter the coast, growing in the cracks and crevices in these rocks and finding a home in the leaf litter and debris. The plants grow virtually at sea level, in the company of alocasias and ferns. Their leafless trunks, often clothed in mosses and lichens, have greatly swollen bases much like the shape of an elephant's foot, gradually tapering up into a branched head of 25- to 30-cm-long leaves, the largest in the genus. From the axils of these rise the racemes of inflated, pouched flowers. *Impatiens mirabilis* is partly, if not completely, deciduous, discarding its leaves when the temperatures drop during the winter months.

The root system is rather limited, but well adapted to the harsh conditions of their environment among the rocks. As a consequence, *I. mirabilis* has evolved an aboveground, tuberous, swollen base, which not only stores an abundant water supply but provides stability to the plant in its often precarious habitat. The stored water also enables the plant to withstand the high temperatures encountered at sea level. This swollen base has earned the species the common name of "gouty balsam," as they grow in an almost perpetually moisture-laden, misty atmosphere, but little of this finds its way to the roots.

Thailand is home to at least five other caudiform species, some of which are yet to be described. A few of these have been known to succulent collectors for a many years. For instance, the caudiform *Impatiens opinata* is similar in many respects to *I. mirabilis*, but much smaller in stature and with yellow flowers. The plants were first found at Pattani in the extreme south of the country, where the climate allows *I. opinata* to retain its leaves throughout the year. Unlike that of *I. mirabilis*, its basal caudex often has multiple stems.

Another of Thailand's caudiform species is *Impatiens kerriae*, found in Dio Chieng Dao in the north of the country. It has a thick, woody, almost shrublike stem, growing to 1 m or more in height and topped off with a crown of light green leaves. Its large pouched flowers are a beautiful creamy white and pink, with flaming orange and red inside the throat. *Impatiens kerriae* was discovered in 1923 by Dr. A. F. G. Kerr, a medical doctor working for the Siamese government. Seed was sent to the Aberdeen University Botanic Gardens, where it flowered the following year. The species was subsequently described in 1926 by W. G. Craib, who also described many other Thai species in the *Kew Bulletin*. *Impatiens kerriae* can be grown outside during the summer months, but it flowers late in the season, so it should be brought into the greenhouse or conservatory in the autumn.

Thailand has many species to delight the gardener, and *Impatiens psittacina* is one of the better ones, found in the more northern regions of the country. At present this species is difficult to obtain, but I am sure it will eventually become more accessible and it is destined to become very popular. The flowers are very an attractive lilac and dark red, and the plant is very floriferous, producing a wealth of blooms throughout the summer. Although this species is native to cold regions, like most other *Impatiens* species it is frost tender.

There are a few more really good annual species, including *Impatiens kanburiensis* and *I. siamensis*. Both are very attractive plants, although their hardiness may have to be proven; when grown under glass, both can be very rewarding and make excellent pot plants. As with so many Thai *Impatiens* species, these are usually found growing on limestone hills. *Impatiens violaeflora* is another annual species offered by some nurseries. It is a shorter, free-flowering plant that produces small purple flowers. This species is also a little tender, so it may also need the shelter of a greenhouse in some places. When conditions are right, the plant self-seeds well.

Taiwan is home to a few *Impatiens* species. *Impatiens uniflora* has been offered by many nurseries for some time. It is a very hardy, perennial plant that only grows to about 25 cm high, forming a neat clump. This species displays a wealth of pale pink flowers throughout the summer.

Japan is the eastern extremity of the natural range of *Impatiens*; considering its many suitable habitats, the country has surprisingly few species. *Impatiens textori* is a small, annual plant, with red hairy stems and lilac-purple flowers. Seed of this species has been available for many years, and it seems to germinate reasonably well.

Impatiens oncidioides hails from the Cameron Highlands of Malaya and grows in warm shady conditions. It takes its name from the color and shape of its flowers, which are quite similar to those of the Oncidiodes class of orchids. This species is very special in that it is the only one producing truly open, yellow flowers. The plant has light green foliage and grows to about 30 cm high. It makes a wonderful pot plant, bearing many clear yellow flowers that are about 4 cm in diameter. Plant breeders have been trying to breed this color into *I. walleriana* hybrids without much success. However, plant technology is moving so fast that it is possible that in the near future this aim will be achieved.

Mount Kinabalu in northern Borneo is home to another fine species. Formally known as *Impatiens platypetala*, it is known locally as the "Kinabalu balsam" and was recently described as *I. kinabaluensis*. Mount Kinabalu is well known for the numerous orchid species that grow there, but it seems that this is the only *Impatiens* species. The plant has unusual lilac flowers, with large, extended, forked dorsal petals. *Impatiens kinabaluensis* makes a wonderful long-flowering pot plant that can be grown both inside and outside during the summer months. It has a great deal in common with *I. poilanei* from southern Vietnam: both species have whorled leaves and similar flowers, but the dorsal petals of the latter are even more extended.

Thailand and most of the adjacent countries have been very poorly researched for *Impatiens* species. Although many have been found, very few have been described. Burma, in particular, is known to be home to a great number of species, a few of which were described in the early 20th century. Little is known about the vast majority, however, and any information about them is fragmentary. This also applies to the *Impatiens* species of Cambodia, Laos, and Vietnam.

The Species

Impatiens species southern Thailand

Caudiform succulent, growing to 25–35 cm high, stems growing from short, stout, woody caudex. Leaves thick, fleshy, alternate, ovate, shallowly crenate, 7.5–12.5 long by 3.5–4.5 wide. Flowers creamy yellow, 2.5 cm long, in racemes of 10–15, in leaf axils; lateral sepals pinkish green, ovate, lower sepal campanulate, with incurving spur; dorsal petal orbicular, hooded, with shallow dorsal keel; lateral united petals 2 cm long, upper pair ovate, slightly reflexed, lower pair longer, oblong, with rounded ends. Seed capsule unknown. This species is found in southern Thailand.

Impatiens species central Thailand

An erect, fleshy, annual species, growing to 30–40 cm high, with few branches. Leaves arranged alternately, glabrous, shallowly crenate, 5–7.5 cm long by 3–5 cm wide. Flowers lilac or pink, solitary, in leaf axils, 2.5–3 cm long; lateral sepals ovate, small, lower sepal saccate, constricted into a short, thin spur; dorsal petal orbicular, 5 mm in diameter, hooded, lateral petals 2.5 cm long, upper petals obovate, reflexed, lower petals much larger, orbicular, 1.5–2 cm diameter. Seed capsule unknown. This species is found in central Thailand growing on limestone hills in Saraburi Province.

Impatiens species northern Malaya

A glabrous, erect herb, growing to 40–50 cm tall, with succulent, branched stems. Leaves arranged alternately, ovate, 5–6 cm long by 3–5 cm wide, margins crenate. Flowers light purple, flushed with white and yellow in the throat, solitary or in pairs, 3.5–4 cm across, membranous; lateral sepals two, ovate, 8 mm long, lower sepal saccate, 3 cm long, gradually narrowing and abruptly constricting into a short, rather claw-shaped spur; dorsal petal cordate, 1.6 cm wide, with no dorsal crest; lateral united petals 2–2.5 cm long, upper pair

Impatiens species from northern Malaya Chuyos Punpreuka

orbicular, 1 cm in diameter, lower pair 1.8 cm in diameter, slightly emarginated at the bottom. Seed capsule unknown. This species is only found in the northern Malay Peninsula.

Impatiens species 1 Vietnam

Lax, glabrous perennial species, growing to about 1 m long, rooting at nodes, stems pinkish red, succulent. Leaves arranged alternately, fleshy, 3–5 cm long by 1.5–2 cm wide, margins serrate, teeth short. Flowers pale pinkish purple, with two yellow spots at the center, flat-faced, solitary, 2.5–3 cm across; lateral sepals two, small, ovate, lower sepal shallowly funnel-shaped, abruptly constricted into a filiform spur, 2.5–3 cm long; dorsal petal almost cordate, slightly truncate at top, 1.5 cm long; lateral united petals spreading, upper pair ovate, slightly emarginated at end, 1.2 cm long by 75 mm wide, lower pair smaller, with two yellow spots at base. This unidentified species is found in the Gia Lai Province of northern Vietnam.

Impatiens species 2 Vietnam

An erect, glabrous, rhizomatous species, growing to about 1 m in height, sparsely branched, stems dark reddish. Leaves arranged alternately, glabrous,

10–18 cm long by 3.4–5 cm wide, top surface dark green, underside pale green, with a pronounced network of red veins, margins serrated. Flowers creamy white, 3.5–4 cm long, in racemes of three to six, in upper leaf axils; lateral sepals four, upper pair linear, falcate, 1 cm long, lower pair ovate, pointed, 1 cm long, lower sepal saccate, 2.5 cm long, gradually narrowing into a thin volute spur; dorsal petal orbicular, slightly hooded, coming to a point at front, 1.5 cm wide, shallow dorsal crest; lateral united petals 2 cm long, upper ovate, lower larger, oblong, slightly emarginated, 1.8 cm long. Seed capsule clavate, 1.5 cm long. This unidentified species is found in the coastal regions of northern Vietnam.

Impatiens species 2 from Vietnam

Impatiens species 3 Vietnam

An upright or trailing, glabrous perennial species, growing to 30 cm tall, rooting at the nodes. Leaves arranged alternately, ovate, 3.5–4.5 cm long by 2.5–3 cm wide, with serrate leaf margins. Flowers lilac to light purple, with some yellow at the center, 2.5–3 cm across, solitary or in pairs, epedunculate; lateral sepals small, ovate, white, lower sepal shortly funnel-shaped, abruptly constricting into a long, narrow, filiform, curving spur; dorsal petal small, deeply hooded, orbicular, 8 mm in diameter when flattened, with a forward pointed dorsal keel; lateral united petals 2.5 cm long, upper pair oblong, falcate, 7 mm long, lower pair triangular, widest at the top, narrowing to a rounded bottom. Seed capsule fusiform, 1 cm long. This very pretty species is found growing in damp places, near rivers and streams, in eastern Vietnam. This dainty species is sure to become a favorite with gardeners for use as a patio plant.

Impatiens species 4 Vietnam

Upright perennial species growing to 30–40 cm high, stems purplish, very hairy. Leaves spirally arranged, pilose, 10–15 cm long by 3–4 cm wide, ovate-lanceolate, shallowly crenate-serrate, shortly petioled or sessile. Flowers in pairs in leaf axils, 3–4 cm across, almost campanulate, light yellow to cream, with orange-red marking in the throat and base of lateral petals; lateral sepals two, broadly ovate, 1 cm long, lower sepal pouched, 2 cm long, constricting into a thin, incurving spur; dorsal petal orbicular, 1.5 cm diameter, with slight

Trailing *Impatiens*
species from
Vietnam

Impatiens species
4 from Vietnam
Mary Sizemore

dorsal crest; lateral united petals 2.5 cm long, upper pair obovate, slightly recurved, 1 cm wide, lower petals longer, obovate, 1.5 cm long. Seed capsule unknown. This species is found growing in the Sa Pa region of the Lao Cai Province of Vietnam.

Impatiens albo-rosea Tardieu

Succulent, perennial species, growing to 25–30 cm high, simple, glabrous in all parts, stems light purple. Leaves 7.5–8 cm long by 3.5–4 cm wide, alternately arranged, fairly dense around the stem, margins slightly crenate, petioles light purple, 4.5–5 cm long. Flowers lilac and reddish brown with some white, 2.5–3 cm across, single in leaf axils; lateral sepals two, ovate, 5 cm long, pale green, lower sepal boat-shaped, constricting into a short, thick, incurving spur 1 cm long; dorsal petal orbicular, 1 cm diameter, lilac pink with orange-red spots at base; lateral united petals 2.5–3 cm long, upper pair triangular, recurved, emarginated at ends, lower petals oblong and thinner, 2 cm long, and curled longitudinally. Seed capsule club-shaped, 1.5 cm long. This species was found growing on the dark forest floor in Cuc Phuong National Park in Vietnam, and it is considered to be fairly common.

Impatiens albo-rosea
Mary Sizemore

Impatiens claviger Hooker f.

Robust, succulent perennial herb, growing to 40–70 cm high. Leaves alternate, ovate-elliptical, 5–18 cm long by 3–7.5 cm wide, glabrous, petiolate, leaf margins remotely crenate. Flowers white, in axillary racemes of two or three blooms, 3–4.5 across; lateral sepals four, upper linear, lower ovate, larger, lower sepal saccate, abruptly constricted into a short, thin, curved, spur; dorsal petal ovate, emarginated, with dorsal crest; lateral united petals 2.6 cm long, upper pair oblong, lower pair longer and wider, with some red striping. Seed capsule club-shaped. *Impatiens claviger* is found in northern Thailand, northern India, and through to Vietnam.

Impatiens dewildiana Grey-Wilson

Glabrous perennial herb, growing to 10–80 cm in height, stems decumbent, rooting at lower nodes, stems simple. Leaves arranged alternately, elliptical to elliptical-oblanceolate, 4–22 cm long by 1.5–7 cm wide, margins shallowly crenate, petioles 1.5–4.5 cm long, with three or more stipitate glands. Flowers white with some yellow in the throat, with lilac or red markings, in racemes of two to four flowers; lateral sepals ovate, 8–18 mm long, pointed, lower sepal deeply boat-shaped, 11–27 cm long, abruptly constricting into a slightly curved spur; dorsal petal hooded, 16–19 cm long by 10–13 cm wide, with crescent-shaped dorsal keel, 3 mm wide; lateral united petals 22–23 mm long, upper pair oblong, 12–15 mm long, lower pair transversely oval, 15–18 mm long, emarginated along inner margins. Seed capsule unknown. *Impatiens dewildiana* is found in northern Sumatra.

Impatiens elephanticeps Grey-Wilson

Perennial stoloniferous herb, growing to 50–100 cm tall, stems erect, simple or branched lower down on stem, glabrous or pubescent. Leaves arranged alternately, elliptical or ovate, 7.5–21 cm long by 2.5–7 cm wide, leaf margins crenate-dentate. Flowers yellow to orange yellow, with some red marking in the throat, in racemes of one to five; lateral sepals elliptical-oblong, 1–1.5 cm long, pointed, lower sepal boat-shaped, with a profile in the shape of an elephant's head with the spur forming the trunk, 4–2 cm long, constricted and incurving under the flower; dorsal petal almost orbicular, hooded, 1.2 cm long by 1 cm wide, with pronounced, forward-pointing keel, green, 8 mm wide, usually pubescent along crest; lateral united petals 2.6 cm long, upper pair kidney-shaped, 1 cm long, lower pair obliquely ovate, 1.5 cm long, slightly emarginated. Seed capsule fusiform, 2–2.5 cm long. *Impatiens elephanticeps* is found in the Kerinci Mountains of western Sumatra.

Impatiens eubotrya Miquel

Glabrous perennial herb, growing to 60 cm tall, stems erect to decumbent, branched, often rooting at lower nodes, with small, darkish, round glands scattered near the top of the plant. Leaves arranged alternately, ovate-elliptical or lanceolate-elliptical, 5–18 cm long by 2–7 cm wide, leaf margins crenate. Flowers yellow, asymmetrically twisted to one side, in racemes of many flowers; lateral sepals ovate, 3–4 mm long, with short, gland-tipped appendage up to 1.5 mm long, lower sepal widely funnel-shaped, constricting into an upward-pointing filiform spur; dorsal petal ovate-suborbicular, 5.6 mm in diameter, slightly reflexed; lateral united petals 14–18 mm long, upper pair elliptical to narrowly kidney-shaped, lower pair narrowly elliptical, 1–1.5 cm long. Seed capsule cylindrical or club-shaped, 1.7 cm long. *Impatiens eubotrya* is found in the northwestern Sumatra.

Impatiens hongkongensis Grey-Wilson

Lax, perennial species, growing to 60 cm tall, rather decumbent, sparsely branched, rooting at lower nodes. Leaves glabrous, arranged alternately, elliptical to lanceolate-elliptical, 8–12 cm long by 2.5–4.5 cm wide, margins shallowly crenate. Flowers pale yellow, the throat spotted with red, large, in racemes of four to seven flowers in upper leaf axils; lateral sepals four, upper pair linear-oblong, lower pair ovate, lower sepal saccate, 2–2.5 cm long, abruptly constricted into an incurving, thin spur; dorsal petal hooded, broadly ovate or semi-orbicular, 1.3 cm in diameter, with shallow dorsal crest; lateral united petals 2.7–3 cm long, upper pair about a third the size of the lower pair. Seed capsule club-shaped, 1.5 cm long. *Impatiens hongkongensis* is only found in very damp places, such as riversides, in the New Territories of Hong Kong.

Impatiens hypophylla Makino

Erect annual species, growing to 50–60 cm tall, stems thin, glabrous, sparsely branched. Leaves arranged alternately, 10–14 cm long by 4–7 cm wide, margins crenulate to serrate, pedicels 1–2 cm long. Flowers pale lilac to white, with dark purple markings in throat, in racemes of five to seven, in upper leaf axils; lateral sepals two, small, ovate, lower sepal saccate, constricting into thin, abruptly incurving spur; dorsal petal ovate, small, heavily hooded, with shallow dorsal crest; lateral united petals 2 cm long, upper pair small, ovate, lower pair much larger, orbicular, with dark purple striping near base. Seed capsule fusiform, 1.5 cm long. *Impatiens hypophylla* is only found at Mt. Tsurugi in the Awa Province of Japan.

Impatiens kanburiensis T. Shimizu

Erect, succulent, annual species growing to 25–35 cm high, pale green, little branched. Leaves glabrous, 5–7.5 cm long by 2.5–3.5 wide, ovate, margins crenulate. Flowers violet blue to dark purple, with a yellow eye, 2.5–3 cm, solitary, in leaf axils; lateral sepals ovate, pale green, lower sepal pouched, constricted into a short, incurving spur; dorsal petal orbicular, 1.5 cm in diameter, emarginated; lateral united petals 2 cm long, upper pair elliptical, spreading, lower pair orbicular, edged purple and white, flower appearing slightly horizontally depressed, obscuring stigma. Seed capsule unknown. *Impatiens kanburiensis* is a very pretty annual, only found in the western part of central Thailand.

Impatiens kanburiensis
Chuyos Punpreuk

*Impatiens
kerriae*

Impatiens kerriae Craib

A caudiform shrubby succulent plant, growing to about 1 m in height, with
few branches. Leaves tending to aggregate toward the top of the plant, alternate, ovate-oblong, margins crenate, petioles 2–2.5 cm long, flowers solitary,
in leaf axils, large, pink and white with flame orange in the throat; lateral
sepals large, ovate, almost orbicular, pink, lower sepal pouched, with short
incurving spur; dorsal petal orbicular, white, hooded; lateral united petals 2
cm long, upper pair ovate, almost orbicular, 1 cm, lower petals longer, forward pointing. Seed capsule club-shaped, 2.5 cm long. *Impatiens kerriae* is
found in northern Thailand and southern China.

Impatiens kinabaluensis S. Akiyama & H. Ohba

Perennial herb, growing to 30–45 cm high, slightly pubescent in all parts,
branched. Leaves arranged in verticils, 7.5–8 cm long by 3–4 cm wide, ovate,
margins crenulated-serrulate. Flowers light purple, open-faced, single; lateral

Impatiens
kinabaluensis

sepals two, small, ovate, lower sepal funnel-shaped, gradually tapering into slender spur; dorsal petal obdeltoid or heart-shaped, 2 cm long, deeply emarginated at the top; lateral united petals spreading, upper petals 1.5 cm long, oblong, emarginated at ends, lower petals smaller, 1 cm with slight point at tip. Seed capsule fusiform, 1.5 cm long. *Impatiens kinabaluensis* is only found on Mt. Kinabalu in Borneo. This is a good plant for the greenhouse; its hardiness has not been fully tested outside, but it should grow well in warmer areas.

Impatiens longiloba Craib

Lax perennial herb, weakly stemmed and branched, growing to 50 cm long. Leaves arranged alternately, ovate-lanceolate or widely ovate, leaf margins crenate. Flowers yellow, sometimes with dark red markings, 5–3 cm long; lateral sepals four, upper sepals linear, 5 mm long, lower pair ovate, pointed, lower sepal funnel-shaped, narrowing into an upturned spur, sometimes marked with dark red; dorsal petal orbicular, 1 cm in diameter; lateral united petals 3 cm long, upper petals orbicular, 5 mm, lower petals 2–2.5 cm long, thin, extended, slightly twisted. Seed capsule linear. *Impatiens longiloba* is found in northern Thailand and Burma.

Impatiens mirabilis Hooker f.

A caudiform, succulent shrub or small tree, growing to 3 m high, stem or trunk columnar, with swollen base, up to 50 cm in diameter narrowing to 35–45 cm in diameter, branched above. Leaves arranged alternately, ovate-oblong, 25–30 cm long, margins crenate-serrate. Flowers 4–5 cm long, yellow, white, pink, or apricot, in terminal racemes of six to 10 blooms; lateral sepals ovate, pale green, lower sepal saccate, abruptly constricted into a narrow incurving spur; dorsal petal orbicular, 1.5 cm, deeply hooded; lateral united petals 2.5–3 cm long, upper pair ovate, concave, lower pair longer, oblong. Seed capsule 2.5–3 cm long, club-shaped. *Impatiens mirabilis* is found in southern Thailand and the islands offshore. This species can often be found in cultivation in succulent collections.

Impatiens oncidioides

Impatiens oncidioides Ridley

Glabrous, perennial herb, with fleshy stems, simple or slightly branched, growing to 30–40 cm tall. Leaves arranged alternately, ovate, 10–12 cm long by 3–4 cm wide, light green, margins crenulate to serrulate, petioles 2–3 cm long. Flowers bright yellow, open faced, in small racemes of three to five; lateral sepals two, oblong, 9 mm long, pointed, lower sepal funnel-shaped, gradually tapering into a filiform spur; dorsal petal small, hooded; lateral united petals 3–3.5 cm long, upper pair small, oblong, slightly upward curving, lower pair much larger and wider, with slight notch at the bottom. Seed capsule 1.5 cm long, ellipsoid. *Impatiens oncidioides* is found only in the Cameron Highlands area of Malaya.

This species is a particularly beautiful plant and the only known yellow-flowered species with flat-faced blooms. It grows well in a shady position in a warm greenhouse, flowering over quite a long period. Attempts are ongoing to cross it with the New Guinea species and with *Impatiens walleriana*, so far without much success.

Impatiens opinata Craib

Thick, fleshy-stemmed species, with caudiform base, growing to 60–70 cm high, sometimes with multiple stems. Leaves arranged alternately, light green, often aggregated toward the top of plant, elliptical to ovate-elliptical, 6–17 cm long by 4.5–10 cm wide, margins widely serrulate, petioles 4–7 cm long. Flowers yellow, in terminal racemes of five to eight blooms, 2.5–3.5 cm long; lateral sepals two, large, ovate, lower sepal pouched, abruptly constricted into a thin incurved spur; dorsal petal orbicular, 1 cm in diameter, hooded, with small green dorsal crest; lateral united petals 2.5 cm long, upper pair orbicular, lower pair longer, oblong-elliptical. Seed capsule club-shaped, 2 cm long. *Impatiens opinata* is found in southern Thailand near Pattani and Bannang Sta.

Impatiens phuluangensis T. Shimizu

Erect succulent herb, growing to 60 cm high. Leaves alternate, smooth, ovate-obovate, 6–15 cm long by 2.5–6 cm wide, flowers pink, with a yellow eye, 2.5–3 cm wide, solitary or in pairs in leaf axils; lateral sepals linear-lanceolate, 6–8 mm long, slightly hairy, lower sepal boat-shaped, with long filiform spur, 4–5 cm long; dorsal petal heart-shaped, lateral petals 2 cm long, upper petals orbicular, slightly emarginated, lower petals much smaller. Seed capsule spindle-shaped. *Impatiens phuluangensis* is only found in northern Thailand.

Impatiens opinata

Impatiens platypetala Lindley

An erect, sparsely branched, glabrous, perennial species, growing to about 1 m high. Leaves in verticils of four to six, ovate to lanceolate-ovate, 5–12 cm long by 3–5 cm wide, serrulate. Flowers bright orange, with small white eye at cen-

Impatiens platypetala

Impatiens poilanei

Impatiens psittacina Weerachai Nanacorn

ter, flat-faced, 3–4 cm across; lateral sepals two, ovate, small, lower sepal shortly funnel-shaped, constricting into a long, filiform, white spur, 3–3.5 cm long; dorsal petal orbicular, 1.5 cm diameter; lateral united petals 2–2.5 cm long, upper pair oblong, 1.3 cm long, lower pair heart-shaped, 1.5 cm long. Seed capsule fusiform, 1.5 cm long. *Impatiens platypetala* is a quite variable species found in many areas throughout Indonesia. *Impatiens platypetala* subsp. *aurantiaca* has been grown for many years; it has proven to be an excellent pot plant for the greenhouse and for summer planting outside.

Impatiens poilanei Tardeau

Perennial herb growing to 35 cm high, branched. Leaves opposite or whorled, 2.5–6 cm long by 2.5–3 cm wide, elliptical-lanceolate, margins serrulate, upper leaves dark green with short hairs, lower glabrous, petioles 1–5 cm long. Flowers pale violet, with two ornate yellow spots at the center; lateral sepals ovate to orbicular, pointed, lower sepal saccate, 1 cm long tapering into a long, thin spur, 3–3.5 cm long; dorsal petal obdeltoid or heart-shaped, 1.5–2 cm long, dorsally keeled, with high rounded lobes, with large point in the center; lateral united petals 3–3.5 cm wide, upper petals oblong, widely spread, 1.5 cm long, emarginate at ends, lower petals much shorter, rounded. Seed capsule fusiform, 1.5 cm long. *Impatiens poilanei* is only found in Vietnam. Its flowers are very similar to that of the Bornean species *I. kinabaluensis*.

Impatiens psittacina Hooker f.

An erect, much-branched herb, growing to 40–60 cm high, with thick stems and branches. Leaves arranged alternately, ovate, leaf margins serrulate, 5–7.5 cm long by 2.5–4 cm wide, with two clavate glands on underside of leaf, near petiole. Flowers light purple and carmine red, 5 cm long, single, in leaf axils; lateral sepals orbicular, light green, lower sepal almost bell-shaped, gradually narrowing into a hooked spur, white, carmine tipped; dorsal petal orbicular, hooded, 1.6 cm across, pale rose colored; lateral united petals 3.5 cm long, upper pair orbicular, erect, lower pair longer, obliquely oblong, recurved, with some red streaking. Seed capsule fusiform, 1.5 cm long. *Impatiens psittacina* is found in northern Thailand, northern India, and Burma.

Impatiens siamensis T. Shimizu

Erect, annual plant growing to 30–50 cm high. Leaves arranged alternately, ovate, glabrous, 3–8 cm long by 2–4 cm wide, margins crenate, with long petioles. Flowers white in center with pale purple on the outside, solitary; lateral sepals four, exterior ovate-orbicular, 6–7 mm in diameter, interior ovate, minute, lower sepal cupped, narrowing into a long, filiform, slightly incurving spur, 1.5–3.5 cm long; dorsal petal obovate, 1 cm long, with short dorsal crest, lateral petals two, 2 cm long, upper ovate, pointed, lower longer, elliptical, pointed, with pale lilac lower half. Seed capsule club-shaped. *Impatiens siamensis* is found on limestone hills in the extreme south of the Thai peninsula and Nalaya.

Impatiens tayemonii Hayata

Erect, glabrous herb, growing to 25–50 cm tall, branched. Leaves alternate, 4–10 cm long by 1.5–3 cm wide, membranous, margins crenate, petioles 2.5 cm long. Flowers yellow with pink to pale red spots in the throat; lateral sepals ovate, 5 mm long, lower sepal saccate, narrowing into a thin, incurving, bifid spur; dorsal petal orbicular, 1 cm across, with conspicuous dorsal keel; lateral united petals 2 cm long, upper pair much larger than the lower pair. Seed capsule linear. *Impatiens tayemonii* is only found in wet coniferous forests in Taiwan.

Impatiens textori Miquel

Erect, annual herb, growing to 40–70 cm high, sometimes with reddish tinged stems, much branched, with reddish hairs on the branches and pedicels. Leaves alternate or sometimes slightly whorled, particularly on upper part of plant, ovate, 3–13 cm long by 3–7 cm wide, margins sharply serrate. Flowers purplish to reddish purple, spotted with darker purple, large, 3–4 cm long, in racemes of three to four flowers, in upper leaf axils; lateral sepals two, dark purple-red, broadly ovate, 1 cm long, lower sepal spotted with dark purple, funnel-shaped, 2.5–3 cm long, gradually narrowing into an involute spur; dorsal petal ovate, 1.2 cm long, with dorsal crest and pointed keel; lateral united petals 2 cm long, upper pair ovate-oblong, lower pair much larger, oblong-dolabriform. Seed capsule fusiform, 1–1.8 cm long. *Impatiens textori* is found in Japan, Korea, and Russia. This species has a few varieties, including *I. textori* var. *pallescens*, which has white flowers, with a purple spotted lower sepal. Seed of this variety has been offered by a few seed firms for many years, and it has proven to be an excellent garden annual.

Impatiens uniflora Hayata

Erect perennial herb, growing to 10–50 cm tall, with winged stems flexuous toward upper part. Leaves arranged alternately, ovate to lanceolate-elliptical, membranous, 1–10 cm long by 1–5 cm wide, leaf margins serrate. Flowers reddish purple, pale purple, or white, dotted with purple or yellow spots inside the throat; lateral sepals obliquely ovate, lower sepal saccate, gradually narrowing into an incurving spur; dorsal petal orbicular or subreniform, 1 cm across, sharply pointed at apex, lateral petals 2 cm long, upper pair oblong, lower pair longer and wider. Seed capsule linear. *Impatiens uniflora* is usually found in pine forests or grasslands in Taiwan. This species has been offered by many nurseries for quite some time. It makes a worthwhile subject for the garden, being reasonably hardy in most places.

Impatiens violaeflora Hooker f.

Erect, much-branched, annual species, growing to 15–35 cm high, slightly hairy in all parts. Leaves alternate, ovate-lanceolate, margins crenate, 3–4 cm long by 2–3 cm wide. Flowers purple, flat faced, reverse side of petals a shade

*Impatiens
uniflora*

lighter, 2 cm diameter; lateral sepals minute, lower sepal funnel-shaped, narrowing to a slender, almost straight spur, hairy, light purple to white, 2.5 cm long; dorsal petal heart-shaped, with narrow dorsal keel; lateral united petals 1.5 cm long, upper pair oblong, lower pair almost the same size and shape. Seed capsule fusiform, 1 cm long, covered in white hairs. *Impatiens violaeflora* is found in northern Thailand, Burma, and northern India.

Hydrocera

The family Balsaminaceae is composed of two genera, *Impatiens* and *Hydrocera*. The latter has only one species, *Hydrocera triflora*, a semi-aquatic plant found throughout Southeast Asia, from India and Sri Lanka through to Thailand, Malaya, and Vietnam. This species differs from *Impatiens* mainly in its seed capsule, which is more berrylike, and in having free, rather than united, petals.

Hydrocera triflora (Linnaeus) Wight & Arnott

Perennial, semi-aquatic herb, erect, growing to about 1 m tall, glabrous, rather succulent, stems five-angular, lower nodes bearing long fibrous roots, internodes hollow, fistular. Leaves arranged alternately, linear or linear-lanceolate to linear-elliptical, margins serrate, 11–28 cm long by 1–4 cm wide, dark green

*Hydrocera
triflora*
Chuyos Punpreuk

above, pale green beneath, midvein sometimes tinged red. Flowers pink, tinged carmine purple, with some yellow inside the throat, in axillary racemes of three to five flowers; lateral sepals four, petal-like, overlapping, lower pair elliptical, obtuse, upper pair elliptical-oblanceolate; lower sepal boat-shaped, spur 6–8 mm long, curved, slightly swollen at the tip; dorsal petal orbicular, 8 mm in diameter, lateral petals both ovate, spreading, leaving mouth of lower sepal fully exposed. Fruit berrylike or pseudo-berry, 8–10 mm long by 7–8 mm wide, pentagonal in cross-section, pale green, becoming reddish with age.

Glossary

acuminate gradually tapering into an elongated point

acute sharply pointed, with an angle less than 90°

aggregate densely clustered

amplexicaudal with the leaf base encircling the stem

anther part of the stamen carrying the pollen

axil point at which the leaf joins the stem

basal at or near base of the stem

bifid split or forked

bract modified leaf on the pedicel below the flower

bucciniform referring to the lower sepal of a flower being saccate or shell-shaped

bursiform shaped like a pouch

campanulate bell-shaped, broad corolla tube in a flared limb or lobes

capsule a dry seed vessel

ciliate having a fringe of hairs on margins

clavate club-shaped, narrow at base and swelling toward the apex

clone vegetatively propagated progeny of a single plant

cordate heart-shaped with rounded lobes at the base

corolla interior part of a flower, the petals

crenate with shallow rounded teeth

cucullate hooded or hood-shaped

cultivar cultivated variety; names noted in single quotation marks (inverted commas)

deciduous plant that loses its leaves in winter or during dry periods

decumbent spreading close to the ground, with ascending tips

dentate with sharp regular teeth

dolabriform shaped like an axe head

ellipsoid elliptical in cross-section

elliptical shaped like an ellipse, oval

endemic confined to a particular place

epedunculate without a peduncle (a stalk of an inflorescence)

epiphyte plant that grows on another plant, but is not parasitic or dependent on the host for nourishment; such as orchids and bromeliads

falcate scythe-shaped, curved and flat, tapering gradually

filament part of a stamen that supports the anther

fimbriae fringe

fimbriate bordered with a fringe of slender processes, usually derived from the lamina rather than attached as hairs (see ciliate)

fistular hollow and cylindrical

flexuous wavy, usually of a stem

fusiform spindle-shaped, narrow at both ends

genus taxonomic rank between species and family; a genus represents a number of species united by a common suite of distinctive characters

glabrous without hairs

glandular with glands, usually stalked hairs with a sticky substance at the apex

glaucous with a grayish bloom, especially on the leaves

globose more or less spherical

hybrid the progeny of two different species or forms within a species

indigenous native to an area

involute rolled inward, as in the margins of leaves in bud

keeled with a ridge along the lower side, like the keel of a boat

lanceolate shaped like a spearhead, widest below the middle with a tapering point

linear long and narrow, with parallel sides

moniliform regularly constricted, giving the appearance of a string of beads or knotted rope

navicular shaped like a boat

nectary part of flower that produces the nectar; extrafloral nectaries may be found on stems and in leaf axils

obcordate heart-shaped, but with the sinus at the apex rather than the base

obdeltoid shaped liked an equilateral triangle, attached at the point

oblanceolate shaped like a spearhead, but with the widest part above the middle

obtuse bluntly pointed, with an angle greater than 90°

orbicular almost round

ovate almost round, but with a pointed apex

panicle branched raceme

papillose covered with small, soft pimple-like bumps of varying sizes

pedicel stalk of a flower

peduncle stalk of an inflorescence

peltate shaped like a round shield, with the stalk at the center

petal generally, the colored part of the flower

pubescent with fine coating of hairs

raceme inflorescence with stalked flowers on a central stem, with older blooms at the base

reniform kidney-shaped

rhizome underground modified stem, often swollen and fleshy

rootstock part of a plant from which the roots and stem arise

rosette encircling ring of leaves

rosulate having leaves arranged in a basal rosette or rosettes

saccate bag- or pouch-shaped

sepal outer whorl of a flower, usually green

serrate sharply and finely toothed

serrulate finely serrate

sessile without a stalk

setose covered with sharply pointed bristles

sinus very deep notch between the lobes, toward the center of the leaf

species group of individuals having common characteristics distinct from other groups; the basic unit of taxonomic classification

stamen pollen-bearing part of the flower, usually made up of anther and filament

stigma sticky part of the flower that receives the pollen

stipitate borne on a small stalk or stalklike base

stipule organs, sometimes leaflike, located near the base of a leaf stalk

stoloniferous producing stolons, creeping, rooting, usually underground stems that produce new plants

suborbicular almost round, but usually narrower

subspecies division of a species in which variants have a clear geographic or altitudinal difference

subulate awl-shaped

succulent fleshy, storing water in the stems or leaves

terete cylindrical and smoothly circular in cross-section

truncate ending abruptly, as if cut off at right angles

tuber swollen root

tuberous swollen and fleshy at the roots

umbel inflorescence in which the branches arise from a single point, usually forming a flat or gently rounded top

undulate wavy, usually of the edges of a leaf

variety group of plants within a species, usually differing slightly, generally referring to natural variations

Suppliers of Impatiens

Plants

Annie's Annuals and Perennials
PO Box 5002
Richmond, California 94805
United States
Tel. (+1) 510 215 1671
www.anniesannuals.com/

Crûg Farm Plants
Griffiths Crossing
Caernarfon
Gwynedd LL55 1TU
United Kingdom
Tel. (+44) 01248 670 232
www.crug-farm.co.uk

Dibleys Nurseries
Llanelidan
Ruthin
North Wales LL15 2LG
United Kingdom
Tel. (+44) 01978 790 677
www.dibleys.com

Fir Tree Farm Nursery
Thesahor
Constantine
Falmouth
Cornwall TR11 5PL
United Kingdom
Tel. (+44) 01326 340 593
www.cornwallgardens.com

Glasshouse Works
Church Street
P.O. Box 97
Stewart, Ohio 45778-0097
United States
Tel. (+1) 740 662 2142
www.glasshouseworks.com

Kartuz Greenhouses
1408 Sunset Drive
Vista, California 92081
United States
Tel. (+1) 760 941 3613
www.kartuz.com

Paul Shirley Succulents
Julianastraat 16
2771 DX Boskoop
The Netherlands
Tel. (+31) 0172 462 480
www.paulshirleysucculents.nl

Petal Faire Nursery
131 Allcock Street
Colbyn
0181 Pretoria
South Africa
Tel. (+26) 012 342 5762
www.petalfaire.co.za

Prime Perennials Nursery
Llety Moel
Rhos-y-Garth
Llanilar
Aberystwyth SY23 4SG
United Kingdom
Tel. (+44) 01974 241 505
www.prime-perennials.co.uk

Seed

B & T World Seeds
Paguignan
34210 Aigues-Vives
France
Tel (+33) 046891 2963
www.b-and-t-world-seeds.com

Chiltern Seeds
Bourtree Stile
Ulverston
Cumbria LA12 7PB
United Kingdom
Tel. (+44) 01229 581 137
www.edirectory.co.uk/chilternseeds

Silverhill Seeds
PO Box 53108
Kenilworth
7745 Cape Town
South Africa
Tel (+27) 21 762 4245
www.silverhillseeds.co.za

Metric Conversion Table

To convert	Multiply by
Kilometers (km) to miles	0.62
Meters (m) to feet	3.27
Centimeters (cm) to inches	0.39
Millimeters (mm) to inches	0.04

Bibliography

Akiyama S., Ohba H., and M. Wakabayashi, 1991. Taxonomic notes of east Himalayan species of *Impatiens*. University of Tokyo, Bulletin No. 34.

Banner, W., and M. Klopmeyer, eds. *New Guinea Impatiens: A Ball Guide*. Batavia, IL: Ball Publishing.

Baskar V. 1995. Studies in balaminaceae of South India. Master's thesis, Mysore University.

Fischer E. 2002. New taxa of *Impatiens* from Madagascar. *Adansonia*.

Franchet M. A. 1889. Plantes du Tibet Oriental. *Plantae Davidianae ex-Sinarum Imperio*. Paris.

Gamble J. S. 1915–1936. *Flora of the Presidency of Madras*. London: West, Newman, and Adlard.

Grey-Wilson, C. 1980. *Impatiens of Africa*. Rotterdam: Balkema.

Hooker, J. D. 1874–1875. Geraniaceae-Balsaminaceae. In *Flora of British India*. Vol. 1, pp. 440–483. Batavia, IL: Ball Publishing.

Hooker, J. D. 1904. An epitome of British Indian species of *Impatiens*. *Records of the Botanical Survey of India* 4(1): 1–10.

Hooker, J. D. 1905. An epitome of British Indian species of *Impatiens*. *Records of the Botanical Survey of India* 4(2): 11–35.

Hooker, J. D. 1906. An epitome of British Indian species of *Impatiens*. *Records of the Botanical Survey of India* 4(3): 37–58.

Perrier de la Bathie, H. 1933. Les *Impatiens* de Madagascar. *Archives de Botanique, Memoires* 7: 1–110.

Shimizu T. 1969. Classification and geography of impatiens in Thailand and Malay peninsula. *Acta Phytotax Geobotany* 24: 43–51.

Vivekananthan, K., Rathakrishnan, N. C., Swaminathan, M. S. and L. K. Gara. 1997. Balsaminaceae. In *Flora of India*. Vol. 4, pp. 99–229. Calcutta: Botanical Survey of India.

Index